MIDSUMMER

A Comedy

by
PETER COKE

SAMUEL   FRENCH

LONDON
NEW YORK TORONTO SYDNEY HOLLYWOOD

MIDSUMMER MINK

First produced at the Theatre Royal, Windsor. Subsequently produced by the White Rose Company at the Opera House, Harrogate.

(in order of their appearance)

BRIGADIER ALBERT RAYNE, C.B., C.M.G., M.V.O.	*Frank Mills*
ALICE, LADY MILLER	*June Garland*
MISS NANETTE PARRY	*Barbara James*
MISS ELIZABETH HATFIELD	*Anthea Holloway*
DAME BEATRICE APPLEBY	*Aileen Raymond*
LILY THOMPSON	*Susan Tebbs*
TED	*Kevin Moore*
MICHAEL HOGAN	*Colin White*
CHRIS	*Bernard Sutton*
MADAME CHAMBERT	*Ann Windsor*
DETECTIVE INSPECTOR WILSON	*Juliet Curtis*

The play directed by NANCY POULTNEY

SYNOPSIS OF SCENES

The action of the play passes in the living-room of Dame Beatrice's flat adjoining the Albert Hall

ACT I
A morning in summer

ACT II
Morning. Six weeks later

ACT III
Evening. Six weeks later

Time—the present

NOTE TO PRODUCERS

If required, the furs and instrument cases in the last act can be changed to others more readily available, and the dialogue altered accordingly.

ACT I

SCENE—*The living-room of Dame Beatrice's second-floor flat in an old-fashioned mansion block adjoining the Albert Hall. Summer, afternoon. It is a charming, faded room, crowded with good furniture (including a grandfather clock), bric-a-brac, and mementoes of foreign travel. There are two entrances, a small door down L leading to Dame Beatrice's bedroom, and double doors just R of up C leading to the hall and passage to the rest of the flat. Directly across the hall is the front door of the flat, opening on to the public corridor. This door has a Yale lock and a letterbox. Up L, large bay windows look out on to the park. The Albert Memorial can be seen in the distance. Down R is the fireplace, containing an antiquated cosy-stove, unlit. Above the mantelpiece a picture on a hinge conceals a small cupboard. Below the fireplace is an armchair, and in front of it, RC, an old-fashioned ottoman with a table above it. A sideboard is up R, with a small chair to L of it. The clock stands to L of the double doors, with another small chair L of it. In the window bay is a flower table. Concealed by the window pelmet is a wooden cradle which can be lowered or raised by a pulley system. Up LC is a large table, with a stool below it, and farther downstage an armchair. Below the bedroom door is a desk and desk chair, and in the wall behind the desk are bookshelves. Above the bedroom door is a pedestal or column with a concealed cupboard in the plinth. In the hall is a hallstand. Three hanging plant baskets are attached to the cradle in the window bay, and are visible when the cradle is "up". A drawing-board is propped up on the table LC with a map of London pinned to it, covered with talc, to which are fixed arrows and coloured flags, and on which are marked various routes in different coloured paints. On the stool below are collecting tins, and cardboard trays of flags with pins through them. On the table above the ottoman is the Brigadier's cooking ringer, clipboard and pen.*

When the CURTAIN *rises, the* BRIGADIER—BRIGADIER ALBERT RAYNE *—aged about seventy, but still with a military bearing, spruce and charming except on the frequent occasions when he loses his temper—is slumped in the armchair down* R, *snoozing. The ringer goes off. He sits up sharply.*

BRIGADIER. Yes, yes, I was listening. (*He looks round, realizes no-one's there and pulls himself together*) Oh. (*He rises to the table up stage of the ottoman, stops the ringer and picks up the clipboard and pen. He looks at his watch, checks the position on the map, then, obviously upset, hurries to the front door and peers out. Dissatisfied, he calls along the passage to* R) Lily!

LILY (*off*) What is it?

BRIGADIER. Haven't any of them arrived back yet?

LILY (*off*) Not unless they've flown in the window.

(*The* BRIGADIER *hurriedly checks the time again, goes on to the bay window up* L, *picks up the binoculars from the plant table and looks out through them. Even more agitated, he replaces them, hurries to the desk, picks up the phone and dials*)

BRIGADIER (*into the receiver*) Is that Swan and Edgars, Piccadilly Circus? (*He listens*) This is Brigadier Rayne here . . . (*Annoyed*) I don't want any department. I want to know whether you still have ladies in your porchway. (*He listens, and answers irritably*) I am not being facetious, madam! One of the Collecting Points of our Flag Day is in your porch: is it still being manned? (*He listens*) Well, can't you go and look? (*The other receiver is banged down*) Here, wait a moment! (*He bangs down his receiver*) Witch! (*He stands fuming*)

(*There are two short rings on the front doorbell*)

(*Hurrying to the front door and calling to Lily*) All right, I'll go. (*He opens the front door*)

(ALICE, LADY MILLER, *enters. With the aid of much help from the hairdresser and cosmetics she manages to look younger than her advancing years. She is always very smart, and very agile though walking with the aid of an elegant cane. Her sharp way of speaking does not hide her amused and gay view of life. She carries a collecting-tin, and a tray of flags— also an umbrella. This she thrusts at the* BRIGADIER, *who places it on the hallstand and comes back to* R *of her*)

ALICE. I'm never going on the streets again! The rudeness, and deceit, and meanness! Even people I know well managed not to see me. (*She takes off her tray and puts it with the tin on the stool below the table* LC)

BRIGADIER (*accusingly*) You never rang me and gave me your position at fifteen-hundred hours, Alice.

ALICE (*taking off her wet mackintosh and handing it to him*) You try holding a tray of flags, a tin, and an umbrella over your head, and see if you could get into a telephone booth.

BRIGADIER (*irritably; taking the mac to the hallstand*) But none of you rang; I never knew where to send reinforcements, or new flags. (*He moves to the fireplace*)

ALICE. Judging from my tin (*she rattles the half-empty tin*) there were too many of both already. (*She sits down stage* L *of the table* LC, *opens her bag and sees to her make-up*) Oh, what a ghastly day. I shouldn't think my arthritis will allow me even to stagger tomorrow.

(*A key is heard in the front door, and* NAN—MISS NANETTE PARRY —*a gaunt, angular, middle-aged woman, with enthusiasm and a deep rich voice—comes in. She is followed by* HATTIE—MISS ELIZABETH HATFIELD—*small, thin, nervous, untidy, bird-like. Both are in mackintoshes and plastic headscarves, carry tins, and have collecting trays round their necks*)

NAN (*taking the key out of the lock*) If I've got five pounds I'll eat my hat.

HATTIE (*passing Nan to above the table* LC *and putting her tray and tin on it*) I don't think I shall ever be able to eat again. I found the whole day most unnerving.

NAN (*moving up* R *of the table* LC *and putting her tray and tin on the stool down stage of it*) How did you do, Lady Miller?

ALICE. Most of them cunningly popped their contributions in before I could see. I've probably mostly washers.

HATTIE. Oh, surely not.

BRIGADIER (*angrily; standing at the fireplace with the clipboard*) Why have you both arrived back together? You were due to finish at Marble Arch at fourteen-thirty hours, Miss Parry. And you at Hyde Park Corner at fifteen-fifteen hours, Miss Hatfield.

HATTIE (*moving above Nan to above the ottoman and taking off her mac and scarf*) I'm sorry, Brigadier, but I simply don't understand these railway timings.

(NAN *takes off her raincoat and hat*)

BRIGADIER (*explosively*) Nothing to do with the railways! It's the accepted Military System.

ALICE. The accepted Military System is too complicated for ordinary human beings, Bertie.

BRIGADIER. Balderdash. The best results in any sphere of life can only be obtained by order and discipline. (*Severely. To Hattie*) And strict adherence to the plans such as I laid down for today.

(NAN *gives Hattie her mac and rain-hat.* HATTIE *puts them and her own on the chair* R *of the double doors*)

NAN (*pacifyingly*) They were tophole, Brigadier; but we found we did better if we hunted in couples.

BRIGADIER (*furiously*) But that wasn't the laid-down strategy! What's the good of my working out exact timings and routes . . .

(*The* BRIGADIER *is interrupted by a series of repeated short rings on the front-door bell.* NAN *moves to above the table* LC. *They all turn to look. There is a rattle of keys in the lock, and* BEE—DAME BEATRICE APPLEBY—*bursts in. She is a charming, exuberant, vital personality in late middle age, dressed for the weather and carrying her tray of flags and collecting tin*)

BEE (*triumphantly; entering to* C) Wet to the bone, but my tin full!

HATTIE (*to* R *of Bee*) Dame Beatrice, how clever.

ALICE (*rising to help Bee with her tray and tin, which she places on the stool below the table* LC) How much of it did you put in yourself?

BEE. Only half a crown. In halfpennies, admittedly, but I wanted to start off with a good rattle.

BRIGADIER. I hope you didn't solicit? Headquarters was adamant that there should be no soliciting.

BEE. Of course I solicited! I shouldn't have got anything if I hadn't. (*Taking off her raincoat*) Anyone who came within reach had a flag planted on them as if they were Everest.

(HATTIE *takes Bee's raincoat, hangs it on the hallstand, and re-enters to up* RC)

ALICE (*sitting down* LC) Why is it lawbreakers always succeed in life? There do I keep to the rules, and what is my reward? A half-empty tin and worse arthritis than ever.

BEE (*taking off her gloves and putting them with her handbag on the table above the ottoman*) Yes, you poor dears. We must have something to drive out the damp. (*Going to the door*) Lily!

LILY (*off*) All right, I know. Make a jug of hot rum punch.

(LILY *enters with a steaming jug, five mugs, and a pair of shoes and a towel under her arm.* LILY—LILY THOMPSON—*is a cheery, forthright, extremely pretty girl with a slight cockney accent, who bullies and spoils them all like children. But her affection for them—especially Bee—is always very obvious*)

LILY (*to* R *of Bee*) Here it is.

BEE. Clever girl.

(LILY *goes above the table* LC. NAN, L *of her, makes room for the tray on the table*)

LILY. I haven't been with you for five years, Dame dear, without knowing what you and the lodgers want after collecting.

NAN (*for the hundredth time*) Not "lodgers", Lily; please.

LILY. "Paying guests", then. Who don't pay enough.

BEE (*sitting on the* L *end of the ottoman; warningly*) Lily!

(*The* BRIGADIER *sits below the fireplace*)

LILY. Well, no other landlady serves hot punch for four guineas a week, I bet.

ALICE. Only four guineas? I've a good mind to move in myself.

BEE. I offered you the dining-room before Bertie took it.

ALICE. I prefer hotels. I'm never going to find another husband if I don't move about searching.

LILY. Dish out the booze for me, Miss Parry, dear. (*She kneels* L *of Bee with the towel and shoes*)

(HATTIE *collects the coats from the chair* R *of the doors and takes them to the hall.* NAN *pours three drinks.* ALICE *rises to* L *of her chair and circles to* L *of the table for her drink*)

(*To Bee*) Come on—give us your feet.

BEE. No, no.

Lily. Yes, yes; come on, don't be naughty. (*She proceeds to pull off Bee's shoes, rub her feet with the towel, and put on fresh shoes*) Did you do well?

Bee. Not badly, considering the weather.

(Hattie *enters, to* r *of Nan*)

Nan. I'm afraid my tin'll rather let the side down. But I missed over an hour this morning; my elocution pupil was late again.

Hattie. Was she any better?

Nan (*moving up* l *of Bee with two drinks*) Worse. I spent the whole period trying to make the poor beast hear the difference between: (*declaiming*) "I'm to be Queen of the May, Mother, I'm to be Queen of the May," and "I'm to be Queen of the May, Mother; I'm to be Queen of the May." It's perfectly clear, isn't it? (*She gives Bee her drink*)

Bee (*ambiguously*) Beautifully spoken.

(Nan *moves above the ottoman to the Brigadier with his drink*)

Brigadier. No wonder you're the shining light of the amateur theatricals, Miss Parry.

Nan. Thank you, Brigadier. (*She moves above the ottoman to* c) But you really may see something soon—I'm angling for Lady Macbeth.

Alice (*with the hidden meaning quite clear*) Then we certainly shall see something.

(Nan *moves to the table and pours two drinks*)

Bee (*hastily*) How did you do with the collection round the flats, Bertie?

Brigadier. Poor. Several didn't answer the bell—though I went before ten o'clock.

Lily. They're getting wise—you overdo it. Must be the fifth time you've been round this year.

Hattie (*urgently; moving up* c) There are so many causes in need of money, Lily.

Brigadier. I caught the film-star, though.

Nan. The one with the flashy flat along at the end of the passage? Good-o.

Brigadier. She was on the doorstep leaving for Venice, so couldn't avoid me.

Alice (*sitting below the table* lc) How much did you get out of her?

Brigadier (*sourly*) Two shillings.

Hattie (*appalled*) Only two shillings?

Bee. It's an insult. The paper said she got over ten thousand for her last film.

Brigadier. Mean little witch.

Bee. I'd been playing with the idea of asking her to help with our poor family at Peckham.

ALICE. Might as well ask her to show some signs of being able to act.

BEE (*strongly*) We must think of new ways of raising funds.

BRIGADIER. If only we could.

ALICE. Yes; I urgently want to start my scheme for helping those living on inadequate service pensions.

NAN (*moving down* L *to above the desk; pensively*) There must be some way of getting money out of people who can afford it.

LILY (*rising, with a warning note*) It was thinking like that that ended me up in Holloway, Miss Parry.

BEE. Lily, we said we'd never mention your—call-up.

LILY (*fondly*) I know, Dame dear. And I'll never be grateful enough for all you've done for me since . . .

BEE (*smiling at her*) It's not been altogether one-sided, Lily dear.

LILY (*softly*) Thanks. (*To Nan*) But I was "in" for taking what people could well have afforded to lose, Miss Parry. They don't see it the same way, somehow. (*With a sudden thought*) But don't breathe a word of that to my new boy friend! (*Looking at her watch*) Oh! I must fly and make myself less of a gargoyle. (*Moving to the doors with the towel and Bee's shoes*) He's dropping in.

ALICE. How exciting, Lily.

NAN. Another one? You're always having new boy-friends.

LILY. Yes, that's the trouble—I can't get one to stick!

HATTIE (*above the table* LC, L *of Lily*) What's this one like, Lily?

LILY. Well, so far I've only seen him after dark. But I'm hopeful! (*She gives them a large wink*)

(LILY *exits, closing the doors*)

BEE (*fondly*) I hope he's nice; she deserves a good husband.

HATTIE. She does indeed.

BRIGADIER (*rising to the table above the ottoman*) Sixteen-twenty-eight hours. (*Winding his clock*) I have to ring headquarters at sixteen-thirty. I'll set the ringer in case I forget. (*Consulting his list*) Mrs Spanager from next door was supposed to bring her tin here by fifteen-hundred hours. Why the devil hasn't she?

NAN (*moving up* L *to the doors, putting her mug on the table as she passes*) The poor beast probably had a hot bath, and's gone to sleep. I'll go and see.

(NAN *exits, leaving the front door open*)

HATTIE. Wonder if Mrs Spanager did well?

BEE. Probably. Few people could resist her lovely South American accent.

BRIGADIER. I find that American gabble impossible to understand.

(NAN's *voice is suddenly heard, loud and urgent, in the passage outside*)

NAN (*off*) No, no! Wait a moment! Here! You! Man!
HATTIE. What's that?

(*The* BRIGADIER *moves* R *of the doors.* ALICE *rises.* BEE *rises to the fireplace and puts her mug on the mantelpiece. They all turn towards the front door.* NAN *enters looking amazed. She carries a large parcel done up in brown paper and string. She comes down* C. *The* BRIGADIER *closes the double doors and comes down* RC)

BEE   } (*together*) { What is it?
ALICE   }   { What happened?
NAN. Perfectly amazing. A strange man came round the corner, dumped this on me, and ran off.
BEE   } (*together*) { What sort of man?
BRIGADIER }   { Did he say anything?
NAN. Not to open it—that he'd be back in a few minutes.
HATTIE (*shrilly; running down stage to* Nan) Put it down, put it down!
NAN (*hastily dropping it in the armchair down* L) Why?
HATTIE (*to* R *of* Nan) It may be a plastic bomb.
BEE. Don't be absurd; why should anyone give her a plastic bomb?
HATTIE. People do give people plastic bombs.
BRIGADIER. Not to people like Miss Parry.
NAN (*indignantly*) I don't see why not.

(*The ringer goes off.* HATTIE *steps back from the parcel with a scream*)

BRIGADIER (*going and stopping the alarm*) Only the ringer. (*He moves to* R *of Hattie*) It must be examined. (*He stands still*)
ALICE (*not moving*) The sooner the better.
HATTIE. Perhaps we should send for the police?
NAN. Fiddle faddle. (*Standing still*) I don't mind examining it.
ALICE. Didn't he say we weren't to?
BRIGADIER (*severely*) If people dump suspect parcels, we have every right to make precautionary investigations.
HATTIE. But suppose it's something dangerous?

(*They all regard it anxiously*)

BRIGADIER (*bristling*) Dangerous or not, we can't dither round it like a lot of old maids afraid to paddle. (*Bravely*) Stand back, everyone! I will tackle it. (*He approaches the parcel warily*)

(HATTIE *suddenly screams and runs towards the double doors. Everyone reacts*)

BRIGADIER. Miss Hatfield!
HATTIE. I'm not running away. Just fetching this—(*she picks up a small rug*) in case anything needs smothering.

(HATTIE *runs to* R *of* NAN, *who is above the armchair and stands ready with the mat. The* BRIGADIER *tweaks the string undone with his pen, and pulls the paper away. A full-length fur coat is disclosed*)

NAN. Christmas!

ALICE (*moving in to* L *of the armchair*) A fur coat?

BEE (*moving to* R *of the Brigadier*) A mink coat!

HATTIE. No!

BEE (*moving below the Brigadier and Hattie and gingerly picking it up*) It is. A very good one, too.

BRIGADIER. Signs of identification?

BEE (*moving to below the ottoman, examining the coat*) No label. (*Feeling in the pockets*) Nothing in the pockets.

ALICE. What about the paper? (*She picks it up and examines it*) No, no writing of any sort. (*She folds it and puts it on the desk*)

NAN (*putting the string on the table* LC) What does it mean?

BRIGADIER (*taking the coat from Bee and moving to the fireplace looking at it*) It means we must act with extreme caution. Mink coats aren't dumped with no purpose.

HATTIE (*terrified*) You mean it's a stolen one?

NAN. Let's try and think. I'd just got to the Spanager's front door . . .

HATTIE (*breaking in*) Don't say it's one of Mrs Spanager's furs?

BEE. No, she only has a poorly cut beaver, a Persian lamb, and a second quality Breath of Spring Mink.

ALICE. You seem to know!

BEE (*crossing down* L) My beloved husband promised me wonderful furs when his ship came in. I knew it never would, but I studied furs avidly, just in case.

BRIGADIER. Well, look closely, and see if you recognize this.

BEE (*crossing* R *and taking the coat from him*) No—(*excitedly*) although, wait a moment! It probably belongs to the film-star.

NAN. That'll larn her to be mean!

BEE. She always has so many men around her that one can't get a proper look. But I'd swear it's one of hers.

HATTIE. But there are masses of other nice fur coats living in the building.

ALICE (*suddenly*) Smell it!

BRIGADIER. What?

ALICE (*moving* L *of Bee and taking it*) Give it to me. (*She sniffs it, then declares firmly*) It's the film-star's.

NAN (*to* L *of the armchair*) How can you be so sure?

ALICE. I came up in the lift the other day after she'd come down in it. It reeked of Patou's "Joy" perfume. So does this.

BRIGADIER. That seems proof.

HATTIE (*to* NAN) But if it's hers, it means it's stolen. Hadn't we better send for the police?

NAN (*taking the rug from Hattie and replacing it*) Why are you so

potty about the police all of a sudden? I thought you were terrified
of them?

HATTIE (*following to* R *of Nan*) I am! But I've even more terrified . . .

(*The front-door bell rings.* HATTIE *screams, runs down stage, snatches
the coat from Alice and puts it behind the cushion on the armchair* LC,
and sits on the chair. She then looks ashamed. There is a pause. The
BRIGADIER *crosses below Bee and Alice to down* C)

BRIGADIER. What did you do that for?

HATTIE. It may be the police.

BEE (*turning away to up* R *of the ottoman*) Far more likely the man
who gave it to Nan.

HATTIE. But if it is the police, how are we going to explain being
found with a stolen coat?

(*The* BRIGADIER *gets* HATTIE *out of the chair. She moves* L)

BRIGADIER (*taking out the coat*) We'll have much more to explain
if we've secreted it.

NAN (*thoughtfully; moving to the desk*) On the other hand, the poor
beast's right. If it's been stolen, we don't want to be found grouped
round it.

ALICE. I agree. (*She takes the coat and hides it behind the cushions on
the* R *end of the ottoman, helped by Bee*) Far better to hide it.

BRIGADIER (*furiously; moving to the fireplace*) But concealment
admits a certain degree of guilt . . .

(*The* BRIGADIER *is interrupted by a firm knocking on the door.* ALL
freeze)

BEE. Come in.

(ALICE *sits* R *on the ottoman. The door opens and a young, tough-
looking policeman in uniform comes in.* HATTIE *stares at him and screams.*
NAN *takes her by the hand and assumes command*)

NAN (*pulling Hattie towards the desk*) Good, dear, good. (*To the
others*) An excellent example of a perfectly produced "Surprise
Reaction". I shall expect you all to be able to do it next lesson.
(*To the policeman, moving to the stool* R *of the table*) Forgive me—just
finishing an elocution class.

(LILY *enters to* R *of the policeman, who is up* C)

LILY. It's my new friend, Ted.

BEE. Oh, what a pleasant surprise! (*She moves to* R *of Lily and shakes
hands with Ted across her*) How do you do Ted?

TED. Nicely, thanks. I didn't want to interrupt, but Lily says I
must come in and be given the once over.

LILY. Don't you believe him. He's so nosy after what I've told him, I couldn't keep him out.

BEE. Well, I hope you won't find us nearly as peculiar as she's said. (*Introducing*) This is Lady Miller, Miss Nanette Parry, Miss Elizabeth Hatfield, and Brigadier Rayne.

TED. Pleased to meet you all. (*He gazes at them curiously in turn*)

LILY. Don't mind his staring as if you was guilty.

(*They all gasp.* HATTIE *flops into the desk chair*)

That's his training. (*Looking fondly at him*) He's shy, really. Been hanging about outside in the corridor for the last ten minutes.

ALICE. Whatever for?

TED. I was early. I didn't want to cause a bad impression the first time by being previous.

LILY. It caused a very good impression—(*snuggling against him*) shows you're keen.

(TED *looks embarrassed and clears his throat. She steps clear again*)

BEE (*pointedly*) You've been. standing in the corridor the last ten minutes or so?

TED. Well, sort of moving up and down.

BEE (*too casually; moving down to the table above the ottoman*) Did you —see anything?

TED. What sort of thing, madam?

BRIGADIER (*catching on*) Dame Beatrice is testing your powers of observation—to see how you're getting along in your career. Tell us exactly what you noticed.

TED. You mean the colour of the carpet, and who's polished their letter-box?

NAN. More "who" you saw, and what they were doing.

TED. Well, let's see. A lady came out of Number Ten—a lady with nice legs.

LILY. Nice legs? Twin rockets.

TED (*taking no notice, and moving down* C *level with the Brigadier*) Probably going away—she carried a bit of luggage.

BRIGADIER (*keenly*) How big was the luggage?

TED. Sort of enough for a couple of nights.

BEE. It couldn't, by chance, have been a parcel about—(*outlining it in gesture*) this size?

TED. No.

NAN. You didn't see anyone with a parcel of about—(*she outlines it in size*)

LILY (*moving down to* R *of Ted*) 'Ere! What is all this?

TED. Can't say I did. (*Remembering*) Wait a minute! I saw a bloke for a moment who might have been carrying something. But he turned and hurried away where he came from.

HATTIE (*rising*) Ah!

LILY. What do you mean, "Ah"?

NAN (*hastily; pushing Hattie into the chair again*) She means Ted's very perceptive.

ALICE. Have you any idea what this man looked like?

LILY. 'Ere! That's enough, that's enough! He's come to have a cuppa with me, not play "who saw what down the passage". (*Going to the door and beckoning with her head*) Come on.

TED (*going to the door*) Well, thanks a lot; it's been a pleasure to make your acquaintance.

BEE. It's been very interesting for us, I assure you.

(TED *exits.* LILY *winks to them behind his back, and follows him off, closing the doors*)

NAN (*in an excited whisper; moving above the armchair* LC) The poor beast he saw must have been the one who gave me the parcel.

ALICE. I wonder if he mistook you for an accomplice who was supposed to be waiting.

BRIGADIER. He'd know an accomplice by sight.

BEE. Even if he didn't, they'd have realized their mistake by now, and been round here.

NAN. Maybe they can't find which flat I was outside—all the front doors look much the same.

(*The front-door bell rings.* HATTIE *rises*)

BEE. That probably means we can stop guessing.

ALICE. Ghastly as it all is, I shall be almost sorry when we know.

HATTIE. I shan't. If this goes on I shall have to take to my nerve tonic again.

(*The door opens and* LILY *appears*)

LILY. Two nuns collecting for charity.

HATTIE. Is that all?

LILY. What do you expect—the whole convent?

BEE (*taking a coin from her handbag*) Give them this, Lily, and say we're sorry it's not more.

LILY (*going to take the money*) Shan't say anything of the sort. They have a lovely time ringing people's bells and glimpsing high life.

(LILY *exits, closing the doors*)

HATTIE (*moving towards Nan*) Nuns! They're probably the burglars in disguise.

BRIGADIER. Nonsense.

HATTIE. The Germans often dropped men disguised as nuns in the war.

BRIGADIER. As you're always telling me—the war is over.

(*The front-door bell rings again.* LILY *immediately pops her head in*)

B

LILY. Ted's going to think we run a betting shop.

ALICE (*rising to the Brigadier*) I can't think why—but I feel guilty.

BEE. Surely this time it must be about . . . (*She nods to where the fur is hidden*)

BRIGADIER. More likely the Gas Board. I rang them—the bath geyser singed me again this morning.

HATTIE. If he's not a man we've seen before, ask for his credentials.

(*The door opens and* LILY *slips in, closing it behind her*)

LILY (*up* C) There's a man to see you, Dame dear.

(*They all glance at one another*)

HATTIE (*shrilly*) It's him!

LILY. Who?

HATTIE (*weakly*) The man about the Brigadier's singeing.

BEE. The gas.

LILY. No, Dame dear.

BEE. Who, then?

LILY. He says you wouldn't know his name.

BEE (*moving to* R *of Lily*) Well, tell him I'm not seeing him till I hear it.

LILY (*quizzically*) I should, Dame dear. He gave me this. (*She shows them a ten-shilling note*)

BEE. Oh! If he has ten shillingses to give away, perhaps I'd better see him. (*After a moment's rapid thought*) Detain him a minute and then show him in.

LILY (*surprised*) Why?

BEE (*giving her a little slap*) Do as I say!

(LILY *shrugs and goes out*)

(*Moving down* C) It suddenly struck me. It may be some sort of confidence trick.

ALICE (*moving to her*) Someone trying to trap us into buying the coat?

BRIGADIER (*nodding*) Possible. These salesmen are up to all sorts of dodges.

BEE. If we admit we have it, we're "involved". We must pretend we know nothing.

NAN. Then he'll go away and we'll be none the wiser.

HATTIE. And be left with a perhaps "hot" coat on our hands.

BEE (*turning away up* C) That's true.

ALICE (*thoughtfully*) We must know about it, but not have it.

BRIGADIER (*irritably*) How the devil can we know about it if we haven't got it?

ALICE. Could someone have telephoned us?

NAN. Mrs Spanager, next door! If he'd dumped it on her, it's quite on the cards she'd have rung us.

BEE (*moving down* C) That's it!

HATTIE. But mightn't this man recognize you, Nan?

NAN. Unlikely; it was all a shemozzle.

BEE. It's a risk, though. Go in my bedroom while we find out.

NAN. Right-o.

(NAN *darts out to the bedroom down* L)

BRIGADIER. We mustn't stand looking guilty. Settle at ease.

(*They all "settle" with various occupations.* ALICE *goes to sit at the desk, colliding with* BEE *down* C, *who is going to sit* R *on the ottoman. The* BRIGADIER *gives Bee her work-box from up stage of the fireplace, then sits down* R *with "The Times".* HATTIE *goes to the window up* L *and starts watering the plants.* LILY *knocks, opens the door and announces*)

LILY. The gentleman.

(MICHAEL HOGAN *enters to* R *of Lily. He is a smiling, nice-looking, youngish man, with an appealing if somewhat conscious charm, and a slight Irish accent. His obvious blarney does not completely hide his present nervousness.* LILY *exits*)

MIKE. Is one of you charming ladies the owner of this flat?

BEE. Why?

MIKE (*momentarily nonplussed*) You have every right to ask. (*Recovering*) And I feel dreadful disturbing your peace like this . . .

BEE. There's no need to feel dreadful; just tell us why you are, Mr . . . ?

MIKE (*moving down stage*) Hicks. Joe Hicks. Well, it's rather a long story, I'm afraid . . .

BEE. Then you'd better sit down, Mr Joseph Hicks.

MIKE (*sitting in the armchair down* LC) You're as kind and considerate as you look, Lady Beatrice.

BRIGADIER (*suspiciously*) You know her name?

MIKE (*again slightly nonplussed*) It's on the card at the front door. (*He looks searchingly round the room. He catches Alice's eye and takes his hat off*)

ALICE. Well, we're all ready for the story, Mr Hicks.

(HATTIE *moves down to up* L *of Mike*)

MIKE. Ah, yes. Well, it's like this now. I was visiting friends in the building. When I got out of the lift I remembered I'd forgot to put sixpence in the parking meter. Where I come from we don't have meters.

BEE (*drily*) We don't here, either.

HATTIE. No, they haven't started them in this area yet.

MIKE (*mopping his brow*) Well, actually it was more towards

Piccadilly. I wasn't quite sure where this building was, so I parked where I saw a space.

BRIGADIER. Wise man. Go on.

MIKE. Well, I didn't want to lose me car—I think more of her than I do me girl—so I gave what I was carrying to a charming lady at her front door, asking her to look after it, and off I flew. Well, I still have me car, but I haven't got what I was carrying.

(*They all gaze at him in silence*)

(*Shifting in his seat, his smile becoming more forced*) You don't seem concerned about me loss?

BRIGADIER. On the contrary, Mr Hicks, we're anxious to know more.

ALICE. Yes, you haven't said what it was you were carrying.

MIKE. Haven't I now? Isn't that just like me. It's the most important part of the story, and I leave it out. It was a parcel.

BEE. Containing?

MIKE (*after a moment*) Clothes.

(*They all gaze at him*)

(*Sadly*) You see, as I'm far from home, and live on me own, this dear friend of mine does me mending.

ALICE. Oh! Mending, was it?

MIKE. The holiest pile you've ever seen! It would have amazed you.

ALICE (*with meaning*) It does!

BRIGADIER (*rising to the fireplace*) When are you coming to the point of this—story, Mr Hicks?

MIKE. Haven't you got it? It's that I want me parcel back.

BEE. Then you're going to be disappointed, Mr Hicks. (*Slowly*) None of us is the "charming lady".

MIKE (*shaken*) But I'm almost certain it was outside this flat.

ALICE. It couldn't have been our American neighbour next door, Mrs Spanager?

MIKE (*uncertainly*) I suppose it might, now; I was in such a hurry. (*Rising*) Well, I most sincerely ask your pardons. I'll go and try the United States. (*He moves up* C, *putting on his hat*)

BEE (*quietly*) You're sure it's mending you've lost, Mr Hicks? Not mink?

(MIKE *freezes, then slowly turns to them*)

MIKE. Mink?

ALICE. A rather nice coat with bishop's sleeves.

MIKE (*moving down* C; *spontaneously bursting out*) How dishonest of you to open it.

BEE (*quickly; rising*) So you admit it's the film-star's coat?

MIKE. Yes. I mean, no! (*Flustered*) I mean; have you got it, then?

ALICE. We needn't have it to know about it. Mrs Spanager, next door, can have telephoned and asked our advice.

MIKE (*quickly*) What did you say? Not the police?

(*The* BRIGADIER *moves above the ottoman to* R *of Mike and indicates to him to sit again.* MIKE *does so*)

BRIGADIER (*up* R *of Mike*) You'd better tell us the truth, Mr Hicks.

MIKE (*after a moment's thought*) If I do, will you help me get it back?

BEE (*guardedly*) We might.

MIKE (*after more rapid thought, and with tears in his eyes*) Well, it's like this, now—I have a wife, Maureen . . . (*He takes off his hat*)

BEE (*interrupting*) As well as a girl friend?

MIKE. Eh?

BEE (*moving to* R *of him*) You said your car was as dear as your girl to you.

MIKE (*mopping again*) Oh, yes, I did, didn't I? (*Inspired*) But you see, I call me wife "me girl"—it's me way of speaking.

BEE (*drily*) I see. Go on.

MIKE. Well, I have me girl—me wife, Maureen, and three children. I've been out of work for six weeks—so we've rather run short of cash . . .

HATTIE (*up* L *of Mike; interrupting*) What about your car?

MIKE. Eh?

HATTIE. Why don't you sell your car and raise money?

(MIKE's *immediate reaction is a baleful look at her, but he quickly switches it to a sad smile*)

MIKE. It's only borrowed.

(*The* BRIGADIER *and* BEE *exchange looks*)

From a very dear and close friend.

HATTIE. I see. Go on.

MIKE. Well, as you seem to know, the coat is the film-star's. (*Quickly*) Is she a friend of your's?

BEE. Only a neighbour.

MIKE (*relieved*) Oh. But you'll have heard of how generous she is?

ALICE (*eyes wide, rising to down* L *of Hattie*) Oh, yes?

MIKE. Well, I did crowd work on her last film, and—I don't know why—but she took a sort of fancy to me. And when she heard about my unhappy financial position, she said she had this old fur coat, which she'd give to Maureen.

BRIGADIER. Does Maureen want a mink in midsummer?

MIKE (*again smothering his spontaneous reaction*) It's to sell—to raise money.

BRIGADIER. I see. Go on.

MIKE. There's nothing to go on! That's it.
BEE. When exactly did she give you this coat?
MIKE. Not a quarter of an hour ago.
BEE. She gave it to you herself?
MIKE. With her own hands. Wasn't that kind?
ALICE. Unbelievably kind!
MIKE. So now will you help me to get it back?
BEE (*pointing to the mantelpiece*) Just pass the remainder of my punch so that I can drink while I think, will you?
MIKE (*rising and crossing to the mantelpiece down* R) With all the willingness in the world.
BEE (*following him to below the ottoman*) Thank you. (*As she takes it, she spills the remainder of the contents on to him*) Oh, I am so sorry. How careless of me.
MIKE (*dabbing it with his handkerchief*) It's all right.
BEE. It's not all right at all. You must sponge it with cold water before it stains. (*Pushing Mike to her* L) Quickly, Bertie, show him the bathroom, and give him one of those useless Christmas present towels.
MIKE. It's nothing—nothing at all.
BRIGADIER (*taking him by the arm to the double doors*) Indeed. Come along.
MIKE. But I wouldn't want to put you out so.
BRIGADIER (*firmly*) It's a pleasure, I assure you.

(*The* BRIGADIER *exits, taking* MIKE *with him. As he closes the doors, he gives the "thumbs-up" sign to Bee*)

ALICE (*in a whisper; moving* L *of Bee*) Clever thing; I was wondering how to get him out of the way.

(NAN *enters down* L, *to* L *of the armchair*)

BEE (*moving to* R *of the table* LC *and putting down her mug*) Did you hear any of that, Nan?
NAN. As much as I could through the keyhole.
BEE (*to Hattie*) Go and beckon Bertie back, quickly.

(HATTIE *flies to the double doors and exits, leaving them open.* ALICE *moves to the fireplace*)

ALICE. Every single thing he said was a lie.
NAN. Yes, the Brigadier said the film-star left for Venice this morning.
BEE. He pinched the coat all right.

(*The* BRIGADIER *enters to* C. HATTIE *follows to his* R)

BRIGADIER. The fellow's a complete bounder.
HATTIE (*breathlessly*) Coming away with the coat he must have run into Lily's policeman in the corridor.

NAN. Panicked—dumped the coat on me—and ran.

ALICE. And now all's quiet, is hoping to charm it out of us.

HATTIE. The wickedness of it. What are we going to do—he'll be back any minute.

BRIGADIER (*in splendid military form*) We must form a plan.

NAN. We haven't time!

BRIGADIER. We must make time. His coming back must be delayed. Undertake that, Hatfield.

HATTIE. Oh, no, I couldn't! How? I can't lock him in the bath-room—he'd think it most strange.

ALICE. Say you've a cleaner that's good for stains, and then upset something over him.

HATTIE. Oh dear—all right . . .

(HATTIE *tears out, and almost immediately tears in again*)

How shall I know when it's safe to stop?

BRIGADIER. I'll cough loudly.

HATTIE. Don't leave me long enough to get involved.

(HATTIE *exits*)

BRIGADIER (*closing the doors and moving down stage* C) Now—what is our "Object"? (*He moves up* C)

(NAN *moves up* L)

ALICE. Well, we can't give him in charge; they'd print ghastly pictures of us in the newspapers looking twice our ages.

NAN (*thoughtfully; moving up and down* L) The film-star's got four fur coats, according to *Vogue*. She can well do without one.

BRIGADIER (*moving down* C) That's true.

BEE (*thrilled*) While the money for it would set up our Peckham family for life!

ALICE. Yes!

NAN (*standing above the desk*) What a spiffing thought.

BRIGADIER. Why shouldn't our "object" be to get hold of the money?

BEE (*moving in to* L *of him*) Oh, I don't think it would be fair to take it all—after all, he did the work.

NAN. How are we going to take any of it? He's as cunning as a cage of monkeys.

BRIGADIER (*sitting on the* L *end of the ottoman; thinking*) We must "extract" it from him somehow.

BEE. Let's think it out. (*Thinking it out and moving below the ottoman to Alice*) We've led him to believe Mrs Spanager has the coat. Could we get her to bring it here, pretending she wants to sell it?

ALICE (*nodding*) It'd be worth his while to pay her something rather than lose it altogether.

BRIGADIER (*firmly*) It would be madness to risk embroiling Mrs Spanager.

NAN (*suddenly; moving* C) The poor beast hasn't seen me! Why don't I play the part of Mrs Spanager?

BEE (*circling to up* R *of the ottoman*) No. No!

NAN (*indignantly*) Why not? Don't you think I could?

BEE. Of—of course, but, er—he did see you when he dumped the coat.

NAN (*triumphantly*) But for all he knew I was Mrs Spanager.

BRIGADIER. Quite correct.

ALICE. I think it's the answer.

BRIGADIER. I don't see any snags. (*Moving to* R *of Nan*) You come here as Mrs Spanager, pretending you want to sell the coat . . .

NAN. For how much?

ALICE. Not too much, or he may shy, and abandon it.

BEE. I know! I'll pretend I want to buy it. That way I can drive the price up.

BRIGADIER. Splendid. But he may be back at any moment. (*Taking Nan up* C *and opening the doors*) Quickly, get out of the flat, and ring the front-door bell in the usual way.

NAN. Right. (*She takes a silk coat from the hallstand*) Can I borrow this, Dame Bee? I'd feel safer.

BEE. Yes. There's that terrible hat I bought for the Guildhall luncheon, too, if you like.

BRIGADIER (*agitatedly*) Go along—hurry!

NAN (*getting the hat from the hallstand*) I'll ring three short rings and you'll know it's me.

BRIGADIER. Agreed.

ALICE. Give us a couple of minutes to collect ourselves.

NAN. Agreed.

(NAN *hurries out. The* BRIGADIER *closes the doors*)

BEE. Oh dear, I'm sure she'll overdo it. I'll never forget the performance she gave as Hamlet's mother.

BRIGADIER (*irritated; moving towards the table* LC) Mrs Spanager's nothing like Hamlet's mother!

ALICE. She was quite good as that American dipsomaniac with the batty son.

BRIGADIER. Yes, her accents are very good—she'll be all right.

(*The front-door bell rings urgently three times*)

What on earth's she doing? That's not a couple of minutes.

BEE. Lily mustn't see her! (*Hurrying to the hall and calling*) All right, Lily—I'll answer.

ALICE (*with a scream*) The coat! She's gone without it! (*She takes it from the ottoman*)

BEE (*going to her with her hand out*) I'll take it to her.

ALICE (*hurrying to the hall and pushing Bee out of her way*) No, no, I can manage.

BEE. But your arthritis?

ALICE. It's suddenly better. (*She opens the front door*)

(NAN *bursts in*)

NAN. The coat! The coat!

ALICE. Here—fold it inside out, in case you meet anyone.

(NAN *disappears again.* ALICE *closes the doors and moves up* R)

BEE (R *of the Brigadier*) We must have him back in time for Nan's arrival. You'd better give Hattie the signal, Bertie.

BRIGADIER (*moving down* RC) Are there any other points we should consider first?

(*The bell rings again, three times*)

(*Moving to the fireplace*) That's still not two minutes—she's mad!

BEE (*calling*) All right, Lily—we'll go. (*She opens the front door*)

(NAN *bursts in to up* C, BEE *follows to* L *of her*)

NAN. What's my name?

BEE. Uum?

NAN. Mrs Spanager's Christian name. We're close neighbours—you can't call me "Mrs" all the time.

ALICE. What is her name?

BEE. Haven't the foggiest.

BRIGADIER. What's American sounding?

ALICE. Sadie?

BEE. No, no—too obvious.

ALICE. What about Mary-Lou, then?

NAN (*doubtfully*) Do I look like a Mary-Lou?

BRIGADIER (*irritably*) Doesn't matter whether you look it—that's what you are. Out!

(NAN *rushes out of the front door again*)

BEE. If the bell goes again, Lily's coming to see what's up.

ALICE. I'll slip along and explain it away.

BRIGADIER (*moving below the ottoman to up* C) Let me give the signal to Hattie first, or Miss Parry'll be here before they are. (*He goes to the door and coughs. They wait anxiously. Nothing happens*)

BEE. Louder. (*She moves to* L *of the double doors*)

(ALICE *moves to* R *of the double doors. He coughs again*)

BRIGADIER. Where the devil is the woman? (*To the other two*) You'll have to help.

(*The* BRIGADIER *conducts* ALICE *and* BEE *coughing as if they are singing*)

BEE. They're coming! (*She runs and sits in the armchair* LC)

(ALICE *sits* R *of the double doors, the* BRIGADIER *below the fireplace. A slightly distraught* HATTIE *comes back followed by* MIKE, *who is mopping his suit.* HATTIE *has an empty witch-hazel bottle in her hand and backs towards* R *of the table* LC. MIKE *follows to down* C)

HATTIE. I can't apologize enough. (*To the others*) A nasty little accident with my witch-hazel. (*To Mike*) Still, nice and antiseptic.

(ALICE *slips out to the kitchen* R)

MIKE. Let's hope the drenching has been worth it. (*To Bee*) Have you decided to help me get my coat back?
BEE (*rising to* L *of the chair*) We've done more. We've arranged for Mrs Spanager to come round here with it.
MIKE. Now?
BRIGADIER. She's on her way.
MIKE (*taking off his hat and crossing below the ottoman to the Brigadier*) May the blessings of every saint pour down on you. (*Trying to hide his anxiety*) Is she willing to give it back? What's her attitude?
BEE. That we're as anxious to see as you are, Mr Hicks!

(*The front-door bell rings three times.* ALICE *comes into the hall from* R)

ALICE (*brightly*) That's probably Mary-Lou.
HATTIE (*at a loss*) Mary-Lou?
BEE (*moving to* L *of Hattie*) Mary-Lou Spanager.
HATTIE. Mary-Lou Spanager?
BEE. Yes! Mary-Lou Spanager. (*She pushes Hattie across her to down* L) Don't be so silly.

(ALICE *opens the front door*)

ALICE. It is Mary-Lou!

(NAN, *carrying the coat inside out, comes in. She speaks gushingly in a very good Southern American accent. The* BRIGADIER *rises.* HATTIE *sits in the desk chair*)

NAN. Sure is, honies! Your lil' old kissin' cousin from next door.
BEE (*going* L *of Nan and taking her hand*) Sweet of you to come round so quickly, Mary-Lou.
NAN. Honey, you's the sweet one to ask me. But then since I've been on this lil' island I've discovered . . .
BEE (*interrupting firmly and leading Nan down* C) Mary-Lou, I don't think you know Mr Hicks? Mr Hicks, Mrs Spanager.

(ALICE *closes the doors and moves up* RC)

MIKE (*bowing politely*) It's a pleasure and an honour, Mrs Spanager.
NAN. The pleasure and the honour's all mine, honey. (*In an*

obvious aside to Bee) Why ever didn't you tell me you had such a pretty friend?

BEE. We haven't had him long. And he's in a hurry—(*warningly*) so let's not wander from the point. What's all this about? You weren't very clear on the phone.

NAN. I wasn't very clear, honey, 'cos I'm not very clear. (*She sits* L *on the ottoman*) When it happened I just couldn't believe it. "Mary-Lou", I said to myself . . .

ALICE (*moving to the ottoman,* R *of Nan*) Never mind what you said to yourself! Tell us what's happened!

NAN. Well, you all know that I'm Madam President of our Animals' Welfare Fund. . .

BRIGADIER. Of what?

BEE. Of the Animals' Welfare, Bertie. You know perfectly well.

BRIGADIER. Ah, yes. Splendid cause. (*To Nan*) Well?

NAN (*pulling Mike down to sit* R *of her*) Well, when I say I'm Madam President, I'm not really Madam President: it's really my lil' old Pekinese that's President. But I kinda stand in for him on account of him not speaking too much. . .

BEE (*turning away to below the armchair*) Unlike some people.

NAN. He's called "Niagara"—because of a lil' weakness when he was a puppy. D'you know . . .

BRIGADIER (*sitting below the fireplace*) No, we don't want to.

ALICE (*impatiently*) Tell us about—(*emphasizing*) the coat you mentioned.

MIKE. Yes, from what they say it sounds interesting.

NAN. As interesting as the light in your eyes, honey. (*She rises to down* C) Well, it's like this. I have an Annual Animals' Fair for my animals. And kind folks donate stuff for me to sell at this Fair. (*To Bee, meaningly*) Don't you think that's good?

BEE. A very clever idea!

NAN. Well, this morning, just after I'd finished my mid-morning orange juice, what d'you think?

BRIGADIER (*losing his temper, rising and moving up to the fireplace*) We're not here to play parlour games—tell us!

NAN. Well, as I was standing at my door—waiting for that cute laundry boy who comes on Wednesdays . . .

(*The* BRIGADIER *throws his paper in the armchair and sits again as before*)

ALICE. Come to the point, Mary-Lou!

NAN. I'm trying to, if you wouldn't interrupt so! Suddenly a man—obviously a keen animal-lover—rushed up to me and gave me this for the Fair. (*She shows the coat*)

MIKE (*appalled; rising*) That coat?

NAN. This selfsame coat. And though I'm used to the generosity of this lil' island, I must say . . .

MIKE (*moving to* R *of Nan*) You don't think it might have been a mistake?

NAN (*indignantly*) I certainly do not. And if anyone suggests such a thing, I'll send straight for one of your Bobbies.

BEE (*meaningly; coming to* L *of Nan*) And we don't want a policeman here, do we, Mr Hicks?

MIKE (*unhappily*) No.

NAN (*looking at the fur*) It ain't straight from Maison Dior, I guess. But maybe all right to wear on a foggy night.

BEE. On the sunniest morning it'd look better than my old skunk. You're going to give us the chance of buying it, Mary-Lou?

NAN. Honey, that's why I phoned you. "Mary-Lou," I said to myself . . .

BEE (*interrupting*) How much are you asking for it?

NAN. Well, that's a problem. If I let you have it too cheap, Niagara would never wag his tail again. On the other hand, it's kinda trashy. What about twenty-five pounds?

MIKE. Twenty-five pounds? Well, it's a lot; but I love animals. I'll buy it.

NAN. Mr Hicks, honey, you's as generous as you's pretty.

(*As she is about to pass it to him,* BEE *intervenes*)

BEE (*moving to below the armchair* LC) Wait a moment! I love animals, too. And I love keeping warm even more. I'll give you thirty pounds.

MIKE (*horrified*) You can't buy it!

BEE. Why not? She wants to sell it.

NAN (*too Bee*) It's yours, honey. (*She starts to give it to her*)

MIKE. Wait! I'll give you thirty-five.

NAN. It's yours, honey. (*She passes the coat backwards and forwards as they bid*)

BEE. Thirty-five guineas.

NAN. It's yours, honey.

MIKE. Forty pounds.

NAN. It's yours, honey.

BEE. Forty guineas.

NAN. It's yours, honey.

MIKE. Forty-five pounds.

NAN. I'm gettin' giddy!

BEE. Forty-five guineas.

NAN. It's yours, honey!

MIKE. Fifty pounds!

BEE (*to Mike*) It's yours, honey—Mr Hicks. (*She crosses to Mike with the coat, then moves back to her former position. Mostly to the others*) I daren't risk more.

(MIKE *sits on the ottoman and wipes his face*)

NAN. Fifty pounds for my lil' old Fair! Why, that's marvellous.

Just wait till I tell Niagara—his lil' tail will go like a chronometer.

BEE. Why wait? Why not go and tell him straight away?

NAN (*reluctant to leave*) But I'm enjoying myself, honies.

BEE (*pushing her towards the doors*) Too much! We'll collect the money for you.

ALICE (*moving to the front door and opening it*) Yes, you be off.

NAN. Oke doke, then. And with so much money for my animals, I can tell you: it's with a song in my heart. (*Singing*) With a Song in my Heart . . .

(NAN *exits, singing gaily.* ALICE *closes the front door and double doors, then moves to the desk down* L)

BEE. Don't be deceived by that song, Mr Hicks; she's a hard business woman. You'll have to leave the coat with us till you bring the money.

MIKE (*sulkily; rising and leaving the coat on the ottoman*) I'll pay now.

HATTIE (*moving* L *of Bee*) But you said you hadn't any money.

MIKE (*after rapid thought*) Well, as it happens, I have some cash on me belonging to a very dear and close friend . . .

ALICE. The same one who lent you the car? A friend indeed.

MIKE (*scowling*) I'll borrow it in the meantime to tide me over. (*He takes out a packet of notes*) Though I think I'll just pay the twenty-five pounds she accepted before you butted in.

HATTIE (*moving* L *of Mike*) I shouldn't think anything of the sort —(*emphasizing*) Mr Michael Hogan.

MIKE (*startled*) Why—why do you call me that?

HATTIE (*holding out two letters*) It's the name on these two envelopes I took from your pocket when we had our witch-hazel accident.

MIKE (*moving below the ottoman*) The dishonesty of it!

HATTIE (*ingenuously; giving them back*) No, I haven't read them.

BRIGADIER (*rising to Mike*) Is it true? Are you Michael Hogan, rather than Hicks?

MIKE (*awkwardly*) Well, yes, I am—I can easily explain it . . .

BEE (*interrupting*) I'm sure! But don't bother. Just pay the fifty pounds.

(MIKE *still hesitates*)

HATTIE. You'd better. We have a policeman in the kitchen who'd be very interested to know why you go about with an assumed name.

MIKE (*scornfully*) A policeman in the kitchen! With handcuffs, I suppose.

HATTIE. You don't believe it?

(HATTIE *runs out.* BEE *follows to the doors*)

BEE (*anxiously; calling after her*) Careful, Hattie!

MIKE (*anxiously; moving to Alice at the desk*) There's something going on I don't understand. Is that American dame working in with you?

ALICE. Can you imagine Mary-Lou working in with anyone?

(HATTIE *runs in with Ted's helmet, to* R *of Mike*)

HATTIE. Policeman in kitchen's helmet.

BEE (*moving to above the ottoman*) A large head, you see. He's a large man. So pay up the fifty pounds.

ALICE. Which we'll see goes to those who really are in need.

(MIKE *scowls round at them.* HATTIE *ostentatiously dangles the helmet.* MIKE *takes out his notecase again and counts out ten-pound notes*)

MIKE (*moving to Bee*) Fifty pounds is scandalous.

BEE (*taking the money*) Nonsense. You'll get at least five hundred on a Canadian wild mink of such wonderful colour and exquisite stranding. (*She picks up the coat*)

MIKE (*astonished*) Where in the name of goodness did you learn about colour and stranding?

ALICE. Isn't she right?

MIKE (*exasperated*) It might be worth five hundred over a counter in Bond Street. But my contacts wouldn't give me two hundred.

BEE (*indignantly*) I bet I could get more than . . . (*She breaks off abruptly and stands with an inspired look*)

HATTIE. What is it, Dame Beatrice?

BEE (*her eyes shining*) I—just thought of something. (*With controlled excitement, to Mike*) Something that'll interest you, I think. How much will you sell me the coat for?

MIKE ⎫   ⎧ Sell it to you?
ALICE ⎬ (*together*)   ⎨ Bee, darling!
BRIGADIER ⎭   ⎩ Beatrice!

BEE (*taking no notice*) Remember, my buying it will save you any further trouble, and probably a considerable amount of danger.

MIKE (*after taking a moment to make up his mind*) I'll take four hundred.

BEE (*indignantly*) I thought you said your contacts wouldn't give you two hundred?

MIKE (*pointing to the notes in her hand*) But I've had to pay you out all that. Still, I'll tell you what I'll do. I'll let you have it for three hundred—but that's me lowest.

BEE (*examining the coat again*) Three hundred for a second-hand coat with such signs of wear! Look—all down the edges here, and on the sleeve where she's worn her bag.

MIKE (*taking the coat from her*) It's not fair—you know too much!

BEE. I'll give you two-fifty.

MIKE. Done! It's no price at all, but I have a feeling if I stay longer I'll be paying you to take it. When shall I have the money?

BEE (*handing him the fifty pounds he gave her earlier*) Here's fifty pounds on account.

MIKE (*handing her the coat*) Thanks. I'll—(*realizing*) but this is the fifty pounds I gave you for Mary-Lou!

BEE (*wickedly*) She's a "very dear and close friend". "I'll borrow it in the meantime to tide me over." Come back for the rest on Friday.

MIKE (*dithering; moving down* LC *and back to Bee*) I don't know what to do. I'm out of me depth. (*Rubbing his cheek nervously*) But I'll be right under the water if I linger. All right, then—it's a deal. I'll be back at the end of the week for two hundred pounds.

BEE. It'll be ready—in used notes of different denominations and serial numbers.

MIKE. You stagger me! (*Stumbling to the door*) To think when I came in I congratulated myself I had a bunch of cosy old darlings to deal with!

(MIKE *hurries out*)

ALICE (*bursting out, moving towards the armchair* LC) I suppose you know what you're doing, darling!

BRIGADIER (*at almost the same time*) Have you gone stark, staring mad, Beatrice?

HATTIE. I simply don't understand what's happening.

(NAN *hurries back, to* R *of Bee*)

NAN. Did you get the money out of him all right?

ALICE (*pointing*) She got the coat.

NAN (*puzzled*) As well as the money?

HATTIE. No, she's given him back the money!

ALICE. And promised to pay him more!

BRIGADIER. Why the devil, Beatrice?

BEE (*calmly*) I had an inspiration.

ALICE. Are you sure not a brainstorm?

BEE (*pointing to the door*) That man can be wonderfully useful to us.

HATTIE. Mr Hogan?

BEE. We want money for all the causes we're interested in. (*Triumphantly*) He can help us get it!

ALICE (*horrified*) But, good Heavens, darling, we can't run round pinching film-stars' coats.

BEE. Of course not! We'll leave all that dangerous side of it to others. We'll merely do as we shall with this coat,—(*explaining excitedly*) sell it at far more than we paid, and give away the difference.

HATTIE (*breathlessly thrilled*) Dame Beatrice, what an idea!

BRIGADIER. You mean—act as middlemen?

NAN. Receive furs and then sell them?

ALICE. Set up as fences?

BEE (*nodding, beaming, and crossing to* C) Exactly! Set up in business as fences!

On their apprehensive excited wonder—

the CURTAIN *falls*

ACT II

SCENE—*The same. Six weeks later, morning.*

The table LC *has been straightened and is set for breakfast. The arm-chair* LC *has been moved to the desk and the desk chair to the* L *of the table. The stool is below the table, two chairs are above it, and the third at the* R *end. An extra chair is in the window. The ottoman and ottoman table have been re-angled.*

When the CURTAIN *rises,* BEE *is sitting at the* L *end of the table, the* BRIGADIER *at the* R *end and* ALICE *above the* L *end. They are happily finishing breakfast.* NAN *is standing on the chair in the windows, watching the street through binoculars.*

BEE. Another *croissant*, Alice?

ALICE. No! My figure. But they're delicious. I can't tell you how I look forward to these weekly Planning Breakfasts.

BRIGADIER. Yes, they were an excellent idea, Beatrice. Allow us to meet together regularly without arousing suspicion.

BEE (*strongly*) Well, whatever happens, Lily mustn't get any idea what we're up to. Her romance with Ted is going along splendidly . . .

ALICE (*enthusiastically*) He's a charmer.

BEE. Yes, but he'd be off like a rocket if they found out we were buying and selling furs.

BRIGADIER. They won't! Now that Lily does three hours every morning for Mrs Newcastle we can carry out all "transactions" while she's safely out of the house.

BEE. Getting her that job with Mrs Newcastle was a brain-wave, Alice.

ALICE. Thank you, darling.

BRIGADIER. Only wish you'd thought of it before. (*Worriedly, shaking his head*) I'm not happy about Lily seeing this man who's coming to buy the Persian lambs this morning.

BEE. Nonsense, we've given him a perfect excuse for coming.

ALICE. You're sure he's safe, Bertie?

BRIGADIER (*nodding*) I heard of him through my ex-Regimental Sergeant-Major. He'd never put me in danger. (*To* NAN) No sign of him, Parry?

NAN (*scanning*) Not a sausage. And I'm sure I haven't missed him.

(*The ringer goes off*)

BRIGADIER (*rising to the table above the ottoman, stopping the ringer,*
C

and picking up his clipboard) O-nine-fifty. That's the end of your watch, Parry. Relieve her, Miller.

(ALICE *goes to the window and takes the binoculars from* NAN, *who goes and sits below the table.* BEE *pours coffee for her*)

BRIGADIER. What the devil's happened to this man Chris? He should be here.

NAN. Perhaps he's got cold feet?

BRIGADIER. Unlikely. The R.S.M. said he'd been passing stuff to small fur shops in Manchester for years. (*He returns to the table and sits, worriedly consulting his list*) Hatfield's late, too. She ought to be back from Collecting Duty.

ALICE. I knew we shouldn't have allowed her to go.

NAN. The poor beast gets so het up if we don't let her take part.

BRIGADIER. But she's completely unreliable.

BEE. She only had to go to Victoria Station, unlock the luggage locker and collect the fur that Hogan had left there. Even she couldn't make a mistake.

BRIGADIER. She could!

NAN. She'll muddle through.

ALICE. I've always said collecting points are dangerous. In future let's get the furs delivered here.

BEE. Certainly not! I should lose the lease of the flat if strange men keep being seen on the doorstep.

(*The telephone rings*)

That's probably Hattie ringing for permission to enter.

(NAN *rises and goes to the desk*)

BRIGADIER (*to Nan*) Take full precautions in case it isn't.

NAN. Of course! (*Picking up the receiver and using a strong German accent*) Ya? Ya. Ya. Vat you vant? (*She listens*) Dis an Austrian friend of the family who speak. Who you vant, bitte? Ya. Ya. Ya . . .

ALICE. For Heaven's sake stop ya-ing! Who is it?

NAN. Please to speak more slow, Mein Herr. Ya. Vait then, bitte; I see if Fraulein zu haben ist. (*Covering the receiver*) It's Mike Hogan.

BRIGADIER. You're certain?

NAN. Sounds exactly like him.

BRIGADIER. Not good enough—it may be a police trap. Ascertain before imparting knowledge, Appleby.

(BEE *rises*)

BEE. Right! (*She goes and takes the phone from Nan*)

(NAN *returns to the stool and sits with her coffee, facing front*)

(*Into the phone*) Mr Hogan? This is Dame Beatrice. What was I wearing last time you came here? (*She listens*) All right, all right! (*To the others*) It's him—no one else could have such a gift of the gab.

(*Into the phone*) What is it? (*She listens*) Wait a moment. (*Covering the receiver*) He wants to know whether we'll handle a leopard.

ALICE. No! Spots are too recognizable.

BEE (*into the phone*) No, we're not touching spots yet. (*She listens*) No, not very convenient. We're rather busy this morning.

BRIGADIER (*rising agitatedly and moving to* R *of Bee*) He can't possibly come here this morning.

BEE (*waving him to be quiet*) I see. Well, if it's only for a moment, you can. (*She listens*) May they pour down blessings on your head, too. Good-bye. (*She puts down the receiver*) He's passing this way later on, and wants the money for the last batch he delivered.

BRIGADIER (*agitatedly; moving to the fireplace*) But he may run into Chris! We can't have buyers and sellers meeting each other!

BEE. They won't.

(*There is the sound of the front door opening*)

Sssh!

(NAN *rises. They all watch as the door slowly opens. Eventually* HATTIE's *head appears round it*)

HATTIE. Safe?

BRIGADIER (*furiously*) What on earth are you doing, Hatfield? You haven't telephoned for Permission to Enter.

(HATTIE *comes in. She has on a hat, a fully cut dust coat and dark glasses*)

HATTIE (*coming down* C) No; I apologize. But there was no point. (*Guiltily*) I'd forgotten the password.

BRIGADIER. Hatfield!

HATTIE. I'm so sorry. In future I'm going to write it in pencil on the palm of my hand. Then in Emergency, I can lick it off.

NAN (*anxiously*) Where's the fur?

HATTIE. Well, thinking it over, I didn't like the idea of openly bringing in another parcel . . .

BRIGADIER (*moving above the ottoman to* R *of Hattie*) You had a formal order, Hatfield! You should not have departed from it either in letter or spirit.

HATTIE. You told us to "Improvise" if necessary, Brigadier. I thought of an improvisation, so I did it.

BRIGADIER. What?

HATTIE. I went into the Ladies at Victoria, unwrapped the fur, disposed of the paper, and then came out.

BRIGADIER. What about the fur?

HATTIE. Hold here, Nan. (*She unbuttons her coat*)

(NAN *holds the end of the fur showing.* HATTIE *slowly spins, and* NAN *draws out the long stole that has been wound round Hattie's middle*)

NAN (*holding the stole*) Clever beast.

HATTIE. All right, Brigadier?

BRIGADIER (*helping her to take off her coat*) Ingenious, I must say.

BEE (*moving* L *of Nan*) Well done. (*Taking the fur and examining it*) Blond Palomino Mink, of a very good quality.

NAN. Smashing.

HATTIE. Well worth a hot tummy. (*She gives her hat, handbag and gloves to the Brigadier*)

(*The* BRIGADIER *takes Hattie's things with her coat to the chair* R *of the double doors*)

BEE. We should get a hundred and fifty easily.

NAN. Couldn't we try more? We paid Hogan a hundred and twenty-five.

ALICE (*at the window*) There's Chris now!

BRIGADIER (*hurrying to the window*) You're sure?

ALICE. Yes, he's carrying a box.

BRIGADIER. Yes, that's him. Quickly—we must stow the Palomino before Lily shows him in.

HATTIE. Yes, yes, we must!

(*They all start hurrying about.* ALICE *gets down and moves down* L. HATTIE *grabs the stole from* BEE, *runs to* R *of the table and tries to hide the stole under it.* NAN *grabs it from Hattie,* BEE *takes it from Nan*)

BRIGADIER (*moving up* RC; *shouting*) No, no, no! (*He blows his whistle*)

(*The pandemonium stops*)

In a proper, organized, military fashion, please. (*Ordering*) Prepare for Disposal Action. First Hiding Place.

(HATTIE *starts to go up* C)

Wait for it! Positions!

(HATTIE *goes to the double doors and looks through the keyhole.* ALICE *goes above the window,* NAN *to below it,* BEE *to* C *of it, standing with her back to it*)

Action—One! (*He blows his whistle*)

(ALICE *and* NAN *let down the two hanging baskets of flowers, showing a wooden cradle that is usually hidden in the depth of the pelmet*)

Two! (*He blows his whistle*)

(BEE *puts the fur in the cradle*)

Three! (*He blows his whistle*)

(ALICE *and* NAN *pull up the cradle*)

Now—settle at ease.

(*They go back to their places at the breakfast table.* BEE *takes the binoculars from* ALICE's *neck, puts them on the desk, and sits at the table* L *as before*)

BEE. Oh dear, I'm quite out of breath. Being a fence isn't nearly as easy as one might have thought.

NAN. But marvellously exhilarating.

HATTIE. Too exhilarating. (*She takes a spoonful from the medicine bottle beside her. To Nan*) Remind me to get a new bottle of nerve tonic.

(*The front-door bell rings*)

BEE. Chris!

HATTIE. Oh, dear—I hope he's safe. I hate these odd men. If only we had some permanent outlet.

NAN. Shouldn't I get the key?

ALICE. Yes, we don't want him to see where it's hidden.

BRIGADIER. Might be wise.

(NAN *rises and goes to the parasol below the fireplace to take out the key hidden in its handle*)

(*Rising to the double doors*) Quickly—he's coming.

(NAN *and the* BRIGADIER *have just time to sit again before* LILY *enters, closing the door behind her*)

LILY (*puzzled*) A man who says you arranged for him to call about a new Hoover, Dame dear.

BEE. That's right. Show him in.

LILY. You never told me you was thinking of buying a new Hoover.

BEE. I don't have to tell you every time I buy something. Show him in.

(LILY *goes to the doors and beckons*)

LILY. The Hoover gentleman.

(CHRIS *enters to just inside the doors.* LILY *stands* L *of him. He carries a large cardboard box. He looks quite unlike a salesman, being a small, ferrety, middle-aged cockney. He is ill at ease at finding himself in such surroundings*)

BEE (*brightly*) Good morning, Mr Smith!

CHRIS (*awkwardly*) 'Mornin'.

BEE. Brought the Hoover, I see. (*To Lily*) All right, Lily, dear.

LILY. Hadn't I better stay?

BEE. No, we'll manage.

(LILY, *disgruntled, goes out, closing the doors*)

CHRIS (*moving down level with the Brigadier*) Have you got the coats?

BEE (*pouring coffee*) Of course.

CHRIS. Well, let's see 'em quick. I don't like being at a place like this. I want to get out sharp.

ALICE. It's all perfectly safe, Chris.

NAN. Though as an actress of some experience, I suggest you carry the box as if there were something in it.

CHRIS (*putting the box on the floor down* L *of the ottoman. Sullenly*) I'm a fur-dealer, not a ruddy film-star.

ALICE. Don't despair, anyone can be, nowadays.

BEE (*moving to* L *of Chris with a cup of coffee*) Will you have some coffee? (*She pushes it at him*)

CHRIS (*forced to take it in his hand*) No, no. I'm just 'ere for business.

BEE. You're sure.

CHRIS. Certain. I told you—I want to get out sharpish.

BEE (*moving back* L *of the table and putting down the cup*) Then we'll show you the coats straight away.

BRIGADIER (*rising*) Mount Security Guard, Hatfield.

(CHRIS *circles to up* L *of the ottoman, watching amazed.* HATTIE *goes to the doors, removes the key, and watches through the keyhole*)

HATTIE. Safe.

(ALICE *goes* R *of the ottoman and moves the cushions.* NAN *unlocks the ottoman.* ALICE *holds it open while* NAN *takes out two Persian lamb coats.* ALICE *closes the lid. In doing so she inadvertently closes the lid on a cushion, leaving it slightly ajar.* NAN *is down* R *of* CHRIS, *who is up* L *of the ottoman.* ALICE *is* R *of Nan*)

CHRIS. 'Ow much do you want for 'em?

BRIGADIER. As we haven't had actual dealings with you before, I must tell you we don't believe in bargaining. The price we'll mention is the price we want. Understood?

CHRIS. And I'll tell you I don't pay fancy prices. Specially when I have to go through this lark. 'Ow much?

NAN. A hundred for the two.

CHRIS. I'll give you fifty.

BRIGADIER. You don't seem to have quite understood what I just said. A hundred is low, and fair—it's what we want.

BEE (*sweetly; moving in down* LC) Though, of course, you're under no obligation. Except not to mention our being—connected with furs. But I don't suppose there's any danger of that—now that we have your finger-prints.

CHRIS (*dropping the coats on the ottoman and moving towards Bee; aghast*) You got my finger-prints?

NAN (*pointing*) On that cup and saucer.

CHRIS. Well, blow me over!

ALICE. We may be what is known nowadays as "senior citizens", Chris. But we keep abreast.

BEE. Wonderful the tips we've picked up watching TV plays.

CHRIS (*shaken*) O.K., I'll give you a 'undred. (*He rapidly counts notes he takes from his pocket*)

(BEE *watches, checking*)

NAN. Good show. I'll pack these in your box for you.

(ALICE *hands Nan the coats*. NAN *packs them in the box*)

BRIGADIER. When we have new supplies, we'll communicate through the R.S.M.

CHRIS. O.K. I don't like it, but stuff's 'ard to get, so I suppose I'll 'ave to lump it. (*Handing the money to Nan*) A 'undred.

NAN. Thank you. (*She puts it in the bosom of her dress*)

BRIGADIER (*moving up* RC) A glass of beer before you go?

CHRIS (*picking up the box and following*) No, a double Scotch is what I need, but I'll 'ave it when I'm safely out of 'ere. 'Bye.

(HATTIE *opens the double doors, then the front door*)

BEE (*in a loud voice*) Bring us a larger and heavier model.

(CHRIS *exits*. HATTIE *returns, closing the doors, and sits up* R *of the table*)

(*Sitting* L *of the table*) Well, that was all quite satisfactory.

(*The* BRIGADIER *and* ALICE *return to their places and sit*)

BRIGADIER (*worried*) He's too nervy. Miss Hatfield's right; we should find some reliable and permanent source of distribution.

ALICE. We got a hundred pounds out of him—that's the main thing.

NAN. We paid Hogan seventy-five. That's only twenty-five profit.

ALICE. Still, we're getting on. Couldn't we send out some anonymous parcels of pound notes? I've a tremendous list of deserving cases—people to whom even ten pounds would make all the difference.

BRIGADIER (*to Nan*) What do you say, Treasurer?

NAN (*going to the desk and picking up a pencil and envelope*) Well, without getting my books, let me see. (*She jots down the figures*) On the first coat—the mean film-star's—we made thirty-seven pounds. That is without expenses.

ALICE. They can't have been much.

NAN. More than they should have been. (*She moves up* L *to between Alice and Bee*) We wasted money finding a buyer. (*With an accusing look at Bee*) Those advertisements in *The Times* and *Telegraph* cost far too much.

BEE (*indignantly*) What could have been shorter than "Titled Lady reluctantly sacrifices Magnificent Mink"?

BRIGADIER (*pacifyingly*) The expense was justified. It was our simplest and most satisfactory method of finding an outlet.

HATTIE. I liked it better than Chris. Couldn't we advertise again?

BRIGADIER. No. Safety lies in varying our Disposal Methods. Continue, Treasurer.

NAN. Next we have three beavers brought by Dame Beatrice's old butler.

BEE. Not up to much. But we must encourage him. One day he may get a job with someone who has really good furs.

NAN. Profit from those should be . . .

(*She is interrupted by the ringing of the front-door bell*)

HATTIE (*nervously*) Who's that?

BEE. All right. Mike Hogan.

NAN (*moving up* C) We'll want more money. (*She halts* R *of the Brigadier*) Shall I get it?

BRIGADIER. Quickly—before he comes.

(NAN *goes to the armchair below the fireplace and takes money from inside the cushion cover*)

NAN. I only want two hundred. (*Touching her bosom*) I have the rest here.

BRIGADIER. I don't approve of your keeping money—there.

NAN. It's only temporary.

ALICE. And, surely, completely safe!

(LILY *enters, closing the door behind her*)

LILY. Oh! The Hoover man gone?

BEE. Yes, his machine wasn't satisfactory.

LILY (*to* R *of the Brigadier*) Good, I didn't like the look of him. (*In a whisper*) Not that I like the look of this one much. Mr Hogan. Do you want to see him?

BEE. Yes, and please keep your views of our guests to yourself.

LILY. Just don't want you to be done—that's all. (*Opening the doors*) Mr Hogan, Dame dear.

(MIKE *comes in.* LILY *exits*)

MIKE. The top of the morning to you all.

BEE. And to you, Mr Hogan.

MIKE. No need to ask how it finds you. I've seldom seen a brighter healthier, more good-looking . . .

BRIGADIER (*rising with his clipboard*) Yes, we are. You've come for your money, I gather?

MIKE. You gather right, General.

NAN (*passing him the cushion notes*) Two hundred. (*Passing him the bosom notes*) Plus one. Making three hundred pounds. Correct?

MIKE (*taking them*) Correct. (*He stokes his face with Nan's notes*) And as welcome as warm. I'm grateful like a plant for water. (*Moving to the door*) Now, if you'll excuse me . . .

ALICE (*rising*) While you're here, Mr Hogan, there's a point we want to make clear.

MIKE. I'm in a bit of a rush.

BRIGADIER (*circling up stage to* R *of him; firmly*) Never mind. Listen to Lady Alice.

ALICE. We shan't go on buying from you if you include so much "rubbish" amongst the furs you bring.

HATTIE (*accusingly*) That mole coat and the two silver foxes in the last batch weren't worth trying to sell.

MIKE (*airily*) You've got to take the good with the bad, my dears.

BEE (*rising to* R *of the desk chair*) Oh, no, we haven't, Mr Hogan.

MIKE (*moving down level with Bee; cunningly*) You have, Lady Beatrice, dear. Remember I know quite a lot about you. Things that—certain people might be very interested to hear.

BEE. Look at us again, dear. Do you really think anyone would believe any story you told?

(MIKE *looks slowly round the innocent-looking group*)

MIKE (*doubtfully*) You look horribly innocent, I must say.

BRIGADIER (*smoothly*) It's far more probable they'd believe any story we might tell about you.

MIKE (*smilingly regretful*) Except that you haven't no facts to support it.

BEE (*quietly*) Are the names of the friends you work with nothing?

MIKE (*sharply*) What friends?

NAN (*numbering them off on her fingers*) Jim Donovan, Edward O'Regan, and that very pretty blonde with the slight lisp.

MIKE (*shaken*) Where in the name of the blessed saints did you get those?

BEE. One of the advantages of age, Mr Hogan, is that one's learnt patience.

NAN. One's content to sit unnoticed for hours in coffee bars just watching and listening.

(MIKE *turns to Alice and Hattie*)

ALICE. One gets pleasure from such simple things, too. (*Ingenuously*) Such as trailing people.

HATTIE. The excitement of catching them prowling round the same place over and over again!

BRIGADIER (*moving to above the ottoman, looking at his clipboard*) Your next big job is the house in Hyde Park Square, isn't it?

MIKE (*horrified*) I simply don't know what you're talking about.

BRIGADIER. The debutante dance there is on the twenty-eighth. Shall we expect the furs on the twenty-ninth?

MIKE (*tremblingly agitated*) Shh, shh, shh, me dears! Don't breathe those details even in here.

BEE (*sweetly*) It's not worth our breathing them anywhere, Mr Hogan. Any more than it is for you to breathe about our—activities:

MIKE (*groaning*) All right, all right—you win, as usual. No more moles or silver foxes. (*Starting to go*) I'm going before you tell me more, and bring on me nervous rash. (*Stopping up* C) Oh, by the way, did you do well with that blond Palomino mink?

HATTIE. We haven't tried to sell it yet; we've only just collected it.

MIKE (*moving towards Hattie; urgently*) But I left it at Victoria three days ago!

NAN. We thought we'd let any possible hue and cry die down.

MIKE. You're mad! No-one'll buy it now. It's hot—hot as hell.

BRIGADIER (*alarmed*) You never told us that when you sold it to us.

MIKE (*moving to him*) It's only just got hot. It's turned out it belonged to a chief inspector's wife.

HATTIE (*rising*) Heavens!

MIKE. She's given her husband such a time that the whole force is out looking for it! I'm warning you—it's not safe. (*He backs up to the double doors and into the hall*) I don't even like being in the same house. I'm off . . .

BEE (*following him up* C) No, wait . . .

(*But* MIKE *dashes out of the front door. They all slightly panic. The* BRIGADIER *paces up* R *and back to up* C)

HATTIE (*running to the window*) We must get rid of it—we must get rid of it.

ALICE (*following her*) We can't make arrangements just like that.

HATTIE (*frantically*) It'd be mad to keep it in the house!

NAN (*moving down* R *of the ottoman*) Who can we get to take it quickly?

BEE. Chris again?

BRIGADIER (*up* C) I can only contact the R.S.M. in the pub on Fridays.

ALICE. That other man who buys so well is on holiday in the Bahamas.

NAN. Could we get in touch with any of those other answers to the "reluctant lady of title" advertisements?

BEE. Not after all this time.

BRIGADIER (*moving to the fireplace; making up his mind*) We'll have to use the "House Agent" scheme.

HATTIE (*moving down* L *of the table*) Oh, no. I've never really understood it.

BRIGADIER. We'll go through it before embarking. Miss Parry, the list of those who answered our "flats for sale" circular, please.

(NAN *gets a book from the shelves down* L *and a list from the book*)

ALICE (*moving above the table* LC) I thought the "house agent" scheme was how we were to get rid of the sable coat next month?

BRIGADIER. It'll work equally well with mink. (*Crossing to* R *of Nan*) Are there any on the list who also show interest in furs?

NAN (*consulting the paper*) Only one possible, so far. A Mrs Foster Adams. I trailed her for two days and she went into several shops that sell mink.

ALICE. Hopeful.

BEE (*moving down* C) Let's pray she hasn't already bought.

NAN. It was only two days ago.

BRIGADIER. We must risk it. Get on to her, Miss Parry, and tell her this wonderful flat has just come on the market.

(NAN *picks up the telephone and dials*)

HATTIE (*moving below Alice to* L *of Bee*) But suppose she likes it and decides to buy?

BEE. We put her off by asking an exorbitant price.

ALICE (*moving* L *of Hattie and explaining to her*) It's only to get her here. We then show her the Palomino and hope she'll fall for it.

BEE. We'll let it go at cost price—that's sure to tempt her.

NAN. When shall I say she can come?

ALICE. Soon as possible.

HATTIE. Oh, do you think it's safe?

(*The* BRIGADIER *moves above the desk*)

NAN (*on the phone, and speaking in a very business-like voice*) Mrs Foster Adams? . . . Oh. Could I speak to her, please? (*To the others*) She's in, at least. (*She sits at the desk*)

ALICE (*sitting* R *of the table* LC) Try not to sound anxious.

NAN (*on the phone*) Mrs Foster Adams? . . . Oh, we wrote to you concerning flats for sale, madam. (*She listens*) That's right, madam. Well, we've just heard from the owner that she *is* willing to sell the excellent one we so highly recommended. (*She listens*) Number *one* on the list, madam. Would you care to see it? (*She listens*) Well, as soon as possible, madam; there'll be queues when we let it be generally known.

HATTIE (*hectically; running to* R *of Nan*) Not too quickly, whatever happens!

NAN (*on the phone*) Well, that really *is* soon, madam! But I'm sure we can arrange it. We'll leave you to view by yourself, if you agree; I'm sure you don't want us hanging about. Very well, madam. (*Looking at the paper*) You have the address . . . Not at all, madam. I hope you'll like it. (*She puts down the phone*) She'll be here in about twenty minutes.

HATTIE. Twenty minutes!

BEE. Lily! She mustn't see her—she'd give the whole show away.

BRIGADIER (*looking at his watch*) Ten-ten hours. She should have left for Newcastle.

ALICE. I haven't heard the door.

Bee (*going to the doors*) I'll see. (*Calling*) Lily!
Lily (*off*) Coming, Dame dear.
Hattie (*moving to R of the Brigadier*) She's still here!
Bee (*noticing the cushion caught in the ottoman*) Quickly, close the ottoman properly!

(Nan *rushes to the ottoman, opens it, takes out the cushion, and tries to close it*)

Nan. One of the screws has come out of the hinge—it won't shut properly.

(Lily *enters*)

Lily (*overhearing*) Won't shut properly? Don't worry, I'll get Ted to have a look at it—he's in the kitchen.

(*General reaction*)

Bee (*anxiously*) There's not time, Lily; you don't want to get into trouble with Mrs Newcastle.
Lily. I won't; I'm going an hour late today.

(*They all react as she goes to look at the ottoman*)

Alice. She pays you very well. You don't want to upset her by not being punctual.
Lily (*examining the hinge*) I told her Ted was popping in this morning, so she said be an hour unpunctual. Oh, yes, Ted can easily fix this. I'll fetch him.
Hattie (*to down LC*) No, no, Lily—I'll do it later.
Lily. I'd like him to have a go. The more he does for me the harder it'll be for him to escape!

(Lily *goes out*)

Hattie (*sitting on the stool below the table*) Disaster!
Alice (*rising*) We must stop Mrs Foster Adams.
Brigadier. She's probably set off.
Nan. Then it's imperative we get Lily out of the house immediately.
Alice. Could we say there's been a message from the police station for Ted to report back urgently?
Bee (*moving down c*) That still wouldn't get rid of Lily.
Hattie (*agitatedly*) We must—or we're sunk.
Alice. I know! Nan must ring up using Ella Newcastle's affected voice. (*To Nan*) Could you?
Nan (*imitating it*) Do you know, I think I might if I really tried —desperately.

Alice ⎫
Bee ⎬ (*together*) ⎧ Exact!
Hattie ⎭   ⎨ I'd never know the difference.
                  ⎩ Wonderful!

ALICE (*moving to Nan*) Ring up from the call-box downstairs and say someone's unexpectedly invited themselves to lunch, and Lily must come immediately after all.

BRIGADIER. But when she arrives there and finds Newcastle didn't phone?

BEE (*to Nan*) Ring her as well. You can easily say . . . (*She sees Lily entering and continues in a louder voice, with hardly a break*) that you can't wear wool.

(*The others look at her blankly. She gestures with her eyes to the door*)

NAN		But anyone can wear wool.
BEE		No, they can't.
ALICE	(*together*)	You're allergic to it.
HATTIE		It's so unshrinkable.
BRIGADIER		But better than all these man-made fibres.

(LILY *and* TED *enter,* LILY *to* L *of* TED. TED *has a screwdriver and a hammer*)

BEE. Ah! Good morning, Ted.

TED. Good morning, madam. Good morning, all. Nice to see you.

BEE. It's not nice for you to see this room still littered with breakfast.

ALICE. Yes, we're very late.

NAN. Disgraceful.

HATTIE. We're all behind-hand.

BRIGADIER (*rising*) Yes. Come along—to the sink!

(*They clear the table between them, leaving on it Hattie's tonic bottle, the pencil and envelope, letters, ashtray and cloth*)

LILY. That's right, go on—make him think I just flick a duster while you do all the real work.

BRIGADIER (*to Ted*) We undertake the weekly breakfast washing up, because with Method and Discipline we accomplish it in half the time.

(*The* BRIGADIER, ALICE, NAN *and* HATTIE *exit with dishes*)

BEE (*following; in a whisper to Ted*) That we do it half as well, with twice the breakages, doesn't come into it, of course!

(BEE *exits.* TED *and* LILY *each close a door*)

TED. They seem nuttier each time I come here.

LILY. Say anything against them and I'll bash you. Though you haven't see nothing yet! (*Going to up stage* L *of the ottoman*) Here's the job we want done.

TED. Easy. (*He takes matches and a penknife from his pocket, and sharpens a match*) I'll plug the hole with a match. (*He gets to work, leaving his knife on the table* LC)

LILY (R *of him*) What night are you taking me dancing this week?

TED (*getting into the ottoman*) It'll have to be Thursday. See it doesn't crash down and bash my fingers.

(LILY *goes above the ottoman and holds the lid*)

I'm on duty every other night.

LILY. On duty for Her Majesty, or with dear little Shirley?

TED (*good-temperedly*) Now, don't start on Shirley again.

LILY. Well, I know you see her.

TED. I've seen her twice since I've been going steady with you.

LILY. And did we hear about it last time? Her lovely pink dress; her smashing new perfume; her white rabbit jacket . . .

TED (*amused by her jealousy*) I never said it was rabbit.

LILY. No, but I do—because I bet it was. Bleached rabbit—as bleached as her lovely stringy hair.

TED. I only told you details because you insisted.

LILY. You never notice things like that about me. (*Crouching behind the sofa lid*) I bet you can't even tell what colour I'm in.

TED. A pink, white and yellow blouse, and a button-up skirt—with a stain on the right side.

LILY (*rising*) It hasn't! (*Looking*) Oh, well, very slight—I wonder how that got there.

TED. Then you have fifteen dernier flesh-tinted stockings—with a three-inch ladder near the ankle of the left one.

LILY (*moving dow* C) It never has! (*Looking*) Damn swindlers: I paid eight-and-eleven for those only yesterday.

TED (*with a grin*) Shall I give you any more "details"?

LILY (*sulkily*) You do and I'll cry.

(TED, *standing in the ottoman, catches her hand and turns her round*)

TED. I'd never look at Shirley if you was near. Even if you were covered in stains and ladders.

LILY. That's meant to be a compliment, I suppose? Can't say it sounds it.

TED. Shall I prove it?

LILY. I don't care what you do.

TED. Then I shall. (*He takes her in his arms and gives her a long kiss*)

LILY (*breaking away, to* LC) That's enough for this time of the morning, thank you. And I'll tell you something, Mr Notice-All.

TED. What?

LILY. Your barber doesn't cut the hair out of your earholes. And you didn't use a new blade this morning.

TED (*stepping out of the ottoman to her*) As you've suffered once, you might as well again. (*He takes her in his arms again and kisses her*)

(The telephone rings)

LILY *(breaking away)* There are times when I could crack who-ever invented the telephone over the head with it.

(TED follows her to the desk, puts his arms round her waist, and kisses the back of her neck)

(Into the phone) Hullo? . . . Yes, it is . . . Oh, hullo, Mrs Newcastle! I never recognized you for the moment. Have you got your hay fever again? *(She listens)* Oh, you poor thing. *(She listens)* Now? Well, no, I couldn't, really—*(looking at Ted)* I'm sort of busy. *(She slaps Ted)*

(TED goes to the ottoman for his hammer and screwdriver and closes the ottoman)

(She listens) Oh, I see. Well, in that case, I suppose I'd better.

(BEE comes in, to down LC, the BRIGADIER to the fireplace, ALICE to above the table, and HATTIE to up R)

BEE *(in an over-innocent whisper)* For me, Lily?

(LILY shakes her head)

LILY *(into the phone)* Not at all. Won't be long. 'Bye. *(She puts down the receiver)* No, old Mother Newcastle for me. Australian cousins have flown in to take a meal off her. *(To Ted)* I'll have to go straight away—I'm hoping to be left something in her will. *(Jerking her head at Ted)* Come on—you'd better not stay without me—Miss Hatfield's got her eye on you.

HATTIE *(horrified)* Lily, what a terrible thing to say!

(LILY grins and exits. TED goes to the doors)

BRIGADIER. I hoped you'd have a good effect on that girl, Officer. I don't see any sign of it.

TED. Give me time, sir. Give me time.

BEE. You think you'll be able to do something?

TED *(shrugging)* You know her better than me, madam. I guess the best we can hope for is that I stop her getting worse.

(TED grins at them and goes out, leaving the door open)

ALICE *(in a whisper)* Do you think Lily was suspicious?
BEE. Not in the slightest.
BRIGADIER. If only they go at once. *(Looking at his watch)* If they hang about, we're snookered. *(Urgently)* We *must* go through the Plan first.

(NAN enters through the front door and moves below the ottoman to the Brigadier)

NAN. Did she swallow it?

BRIGADIER. Hook, line and sinker. Well done.

BEE. Did you ring Mrs Newcastle, too?

NAN (*nodding*) First.

ALICE. How's she going to explain to Lily that there aren't any Australians?

NAN. I said it was all to do with trying to get Lily a husband.

ALICE. She'll easily think of something, then; she's spent years plotting how to get herself another.

(LILY *pops her head in*)

LILY. Me and the Law's off. 'Bye.

(LILY *retires to the hall and can be seen going out of the front door with* TED)

BEE. Good-bye.

ALICE (*moving to* L *of the double doors*) Give my lukewarm love to Mrs Newcastle.

LILY. Right-o. Don't get up to any mischief!

(LILY *and* TED *exit*)

BRIGADIER. Latch, Hatfield.

(HATTIE *flies to the front door, drops the latch, then re-enters, closing the double doors*)

Ten-one-seven hours. (*He goes above the ottoman to the ringer*) Mrs Foster Adams is due in about ten minutes. (*Setting the ringer*) Just time for Briefing. Settle round.

(*The* BRIGADIER *takes the clipboard and plans from the ottoman table and sits up* R *of the table* LC. HATTIE *sits* R *of it*, ALICE *up* L *of it*, BEE L *of it*. NAN *sits on the ottoman*, L *end*)

Pay close attention, please. Disposal Operation for this morning. We'll run through it on the military formula as usual, so that there's no muddle or omission. Each of you will explain in turn.

HATTIE (*apprehensively*) Oh dear, will we?

BRIGADIER (*firmly*) Yes, we will. First, "Information". Expound, Miller.

ALICE (*standing*) Information is in two parts. First, "Own Troops".

BRIGADIER (*annoyed*) No, no! First: "Enemy Troops". Who are they, Appleby?

BEE (*rising*) Mrs Foster Adams, who is due here at half past ten.

BRIGADIER (*angrily*) Ten-thirty hours!

BEE. Ten-thirty hours. She will arrive in order to look over this flat which she believes is for sale. (*She sits*)

HATTIE. I'm sure she'll smell a rat.

BRIGADIER (*severely*) No defeatist talk, please! "Information, Own Troops", Hatfield?

HATTIE (*rising*) Us!

BRIGADIER. Correct.

(HATTIE *sits*)

"Intention", Parry?

NAN (*rising*) To get Enemy—said Mrs Foster Adams—to buy mink stole—(*she points to the pelmet where it is hidden*) for the sum of a hundred and fifty pounds. (*She sits*)

BRIGADIER. "Method", Hatfield?

HATTIE (*nervously; rising*) Oh, dear!

ALICE (*in a whisper*) Courage, darling.

BRIGADIER (*irritably*) Come along—it's perfectly simple; deal with the task allotted to each troop in logical sequence.

HATTIE. Well—so that she shan't be able to trace this flat or occupants afterwards—we all change places and pretend to be who we aren't.

BRIGADIER (*nodding*) Known as "Confusing the Enemy".

HATTIE. If she's anything like me, it'll work wonderfully. (*Continuing "Orders"*) Dame Beatrice is going to pretend to be the maid . . .

BRIGADIER (*correcting*) Appleby will assume role of domestic. Continue.

HATTIE. After passing Enemy into stronghold, she remains in hall as "Floating Reserve". Ready to dash to any Danger Point.

BEE. Pray heaven I'm allowed to float calmly.

(HATTIE *sits*)

BRIGADIER. Continue, Miller.

ALICE (*rising and pointing to Nan*) Parry will assume role of Owner of Flat—to further confuse Mrs F.A. She will also assume a French accent.

NAN (*immediately assuming a French accent, and rising*) Oui, oui, oui. I cannot promise that it will be exactly Parisienne, but I shall . . .

BRIGADIER (*interrupting*) All right, all right!

(NAN *and* ALICE *sit*)

(*Explaining*) The Object of all this is so that we're completely unsuspected if anyone should later try to find the flat belonging to a Frenchwoman with an old maid.

BEE (*indignantly*) Old maid!

BRIGADIER (*correcting*) A domestic approaching maturity. Continue, Appleby.

BEE (*rising*) Miller will mount sentry, at that window, throughout operation. She will assume the role of a birdwatcher, so that in the event of awkward questions she can distract attention. (*She sits*)

BRIGADIER. Hatfield's task, Miller?

ALICE (*rising*) At the appropriate moment, Parry will find an excuse to ring that handbell. (*She points to one on the desk*) On hearing

D

it, Hatfield will enter with the mink stole, casually mentioning that she wants to sell it.

BEE. Then we pray.

(ALICE *sits*)

BRIGADIER. My task, Hatfield?

HATTIE (*rising*) You're going to pretend . . .

BRIGADIER. "Will" pretend. The future imperative must be used in orders.

HATTIE. You will pretend to be—(*swallowing*) my husband. You will adopt a mean and bullying attitude towards me. This will give me an excuse to ask for payment in cash rather than by cheque.

BRIGADIER. Very good, Hatfield—well done.

HATTIE (*sitting*) I think I'm getting the hang of it. One just puts it in the most complicated way possible.

BRIGADIER (*furiously*) Hatfield!

(HATTIE *is saved by the ringer going off*)

(*Jumping up agitatedly*) Zero minus five. We must commence operations. Appleby, don camouflage immediately.

BEE. Won't take a moment.

(BEE *hurries out to the bedroom down* L, *while the others bustle about. The* BRIGADIER *gathers up his papers and puts them back on the clipboard*)

ALICE. I must get my props ready. (*She hurries to the window and puts the chair into position*)

HATTIE. I haven't even decided what to wear yet! I've nothing really wifely.

(HATTIE *runs out*)

NAN (*hastily fetching a rug from the chair down* R *and putting it on the ottoman*) I needn't change. Being an invalid I shall be covered with my rug.

ALICE (*moving to* L *of the Brigadier at the table*) I don't think I need camouflage, Bertie. I shall sit with my back to the room most of the time.

BRIGADIER. I wish everyone wouldn't dash about like a henyard.

(BEE *hurries back, to down* LC. *She has removed her jewellery and has on a small apron over her plain dress, a maid's cap on her head, and steel-rimmed glasses on her nose*)

BEE. All right?

ALICE. Perfect, darling! You remind me of . . .

BRIGADIER (*explosively*) Never mind who she reminds you of.

BEE. Can hardly see a thing through these—they were my grandmother's—but aren't they lovely?

(HATTIE *hurries back to up* C. *She wears a lot of chiffon scarves, gloves and dark glasses*)

HATTIE. Will I pass?

BRIGADIER (*circling below Hattie to* R *of her*) No, no, no, Hatfield! You can't wear those dark glasses.

HATTIE. I feel so much safer behind them, Brigadier.

BRIGADIER. Safety lies in strict asherence to the Plans, not in obvious disguise.

HATTIE (*crossing above him to up* R, *putting the glasses in her bag*) Oh, dear.

BRIGADIER (*moving a little down* C) Quartermaster?

NAN. Sir?

BRIGADIER. Issue Equipment.

(NAN *moves to the small cupboard behind the picture over the fireplace*)

NAN (*taking the things out*) All ready, sir.

BRIGADIER. Appleby.

(BEE *moves below the ottoman to accept her props*)

NAN. Your duster, polish, false number for door and false name-card for door—in the name of Heloise Dupont.

HATTIE (*moving to* R *of the Brigadier*) I'm sorry, I know I'm silly, but who is Heloise Dupont?

BRIGADIER (*testily*) The owner of the flat!

NAN. Me.

HATTIE. Oh, yes, of course. (*She moves back up* RC, *mumbling the name*)

BRIGADIER (*looking at his watch*) Zero minus three. She may be early. Take up your post, Appleby.

BEE. Right.

BRIGADIER. Switch off hall light, so that she sees as little of the rest of the flat as possible.

(BEE *nods, goes out, leaving the double doors open, and can be seen switching off the hall light. She opens the front door, unhooks the real number, and hooks on the false one. Then she puts the false card over the real one. She watches the passage while pretending to polish the letter-box*)

(*In the meantime*) Issue remainder of Equipment.

(NAN *crosses to the desk*)

Miller.

(ALICE *goes to* R *of Nan*)

NAN (*taking binoculars from the top of the desk and a notebook with pencil attached from a drawer*) Your binoculars and notebook.

ALICE. Why a notebook?

BRIGADIER. To jot down your bird observations—you're keen.

ALICE (*sighing, as she goes to the window*) I wish I were.

NAN (*taking a monocle from a drawer*) Your monocle, Brigadier. (*She goes to a pedestal up* L *and takes a bank statement out of a secret cupboard in the plinth*) And your false bank statement.

BRIGADIER (*going to Nan and taking them*) Acknowledged. (*He screws the monocle into position*)

NAN (*taking a bell from the top of the desk and a lace scarf from a drawer*) Signal-bell and lace for me. All Equipment issued, sir.

BRIGADIER. Good. Now a final word of warning . . .

HATTIE (*interrupting hysterically; running down* C) I haven't got my Equipment! The mink stole!

NAN. Blast!

BRIGADIER. Positions!

(NAN *goes down stage of the windows,* ALICE *up stage.* BEE *enters to up* C)

(*Blowing his whistle and moving up* LC) Action!

(NAN *and* ALICE *try to let down the cradle*)

NAN. Blast! It's stuck.

HATTIE (*running up and down* C) No! Disaster!

BRIGADIER. Pull, pull!

NAN. We are. Any more and the cords will break.

BEE. Have we time to get the ladder from the cellar?

BRIGADIER. No, no.

ALICE. Try wiggling it.

BRIGADIER (*mounting the chair*) Careful, or you'll have the whole thing down.

HATTIE. It's awful—Mrs F.A. will arrive and we'll have nothing to sell.

BRIGADIER. Shh! (*Stretching*) Can't reach. (*Looking round*) We must put something on the chair.

BEE. You'll break your neck.

ALICE. Wait! It clicked—I think it's all right. Yes!

(*They let the cradle down*)

HATTIE. Thank heavens!

(*The* BRIGADIER *takes out the fur and they pull the cradle back into position*)

BRIGADIER (*moving to Hattie with the fur*) Now don't let this little setback unnerve you in any way . . .

(*The front-door bell rings*)

HATTIE (*almost screaming*) Mrs F.A.!

(*They all slightly panic*)

BRIGADIER (*angrily; to Bee*) You shouldn't have deserted your post. (*To the others*) Quickly, quickly. Positions!

(HATTIE *runs out of the room.* BEE *goes to* R *of the ottoman.* NAN *gets her bell and lace from the desk and lies on the ottoman.* ALICE *sits in the chair at the window, with binoculars at the ready.* BEE *takes the lace scarf from Nan and spreads it inadvertently over her. The* BRIGADIER *spreads the rug over Nan, then hurriedly inspects the result*)

All correct. Action! Let her in.

(*The* BRIGADIER *hurries out.* BEE *goes to the front door and opens it. To her horror* TED *comes in*)

TED. Why's there another number on the door? (*Seeing Bee in uniform*) Dame Beatrice! (*He comes into the room and looks in amazement at the prostrate figure in the black lace, who lies looking horribly guilty*) Miss Parry!

(ALICE *rises*)

NAN (*helplessly; lifting the lace from her face*) You wonder why we're like this?
TED (*moving down stage*) Yes. What's up?

(*There is a nasty pause*)

BEE (*coming down to* L *of Ted*) It's a surprise, Ted. (*Inspired*) For Lily's birthday.
TED. Oh. What?
BEE. Well—I think it's better you don't know—then you won't be tempted to tell her.
TED. That's true.
ALICE (*hastily*) Yes! Why have you come, Ted?
TED. To fetch my knife—I left it when I did the hinge.
BEE. Oh. (*She pushes Ted across her to the table* LC)

(TED *picks up his knife*)

Then take it, and be off—there's a dear boy. (*Taking him by the arm to the door*) We want to go on preparing the—surprise.
TED. Right. (*He goes to the door*)
ALICE. Remember—don't say anything to Lily.
TED (*with a wink*) Mum's the word.

(TED *exits, closing the front door behind him*)

BEE (*shaking her head*) I somehow fear he's never going to get to the top of his profession.

(NAN *rises and gets another cushion from the armchair down* R)

ALICE. Yes, thank goodness he has more looks than brains.

(*The* BRIGADIER *and* HATTIE *hurry on. He goes up* C, HATTIE *to up* RC)

BRIGADIER. Quickly, see if he's really gone.

BEE (*opening the front door a crack and peering off*) Yes; he's going down the stairs.
BRIGADIER. Good. Keep permanent watch.

(BEE *rubs the letter-box while watching*)

HATTIE (*nervously*) That's twice things have gone wrong—what'll be the third?
ALICE. Why don't you take a spoon of your nerve tonic?
HATTIE. I daren't. I'm practically a drug-fiend as it is.

(BEE *rushes in and speaks in an urgent whisper*)

BEE. Look out! Unknown female getting out of lift.

(BEE *dashes back to the front door*)

HATTIE. The Enemy!
ALICE. Heavens!
BRIGADIER. Action Stations!

(*The* BRIGADIER *and* HATTIE *disappear into the hall, closing the door.* ALICE *sits in the chair at the window, with binoculars at the ready.* NAN *lies on the sofa, covering her lower half with the rug. She then puts the black lace over her head*)

ALICE. I meant to read up about birds. I hardly know a sparrow from a robin.
NAN. I meant to practice my French. (*Lying back and speaking with a strong accent*) But I am an invalid. Should I get into any sort of difficulty, I shall cough. (*She coughs*)
ALICE. Don't overdo it, Dame aux Camellias.

(BEE *hurries in, closing the door*)

BEE (*in an agitated whisper*) It's not Mrs F.A.!
NAN (*sitting up*) What!
ALICE (*rising*) Who is it, then?
BEE. She's sent a friend.
NAN. No!
ALICE (*moving to the desk*) Botheration.
NAN. We must work on her, then.
BEE. Yes, but she's French!!
NAN (*horrified*) What! She'll know I'm not in a jiffy.
ALICE (*moving back to the windows*) You must be something else. Italian.
NAN (*frantically*) I only know about three words of Italian.
BEE. You'll have to spin them out. I daren't keep her in the hall any longer.

(ALICE *sits in the window*)

(*Opening the doors and standing* L *of them*) The Contessa will see you now, madam. (*Announcing*) Madame Chambert, Contessa.

(MADAME CHAMBERT *comes in. She is an elegantly dressed, sharply spoken woman of about forty, with a strong French accent. She carries a typed list.* BEE *hangs about in the background*)

CHAMBERT. Good morning.

NAN (*faintly*) Bon giorno.

CHAMBERT. Mrs Adams is unwell . . .

NAN. Trieste. But me, too . . . (*She coughs*)

CHAMBERT. She asked me to come and look at the apartment instead.

NAN. Disastro!

CHAMBERT (*sharply*) I beg your pardon?

ALICE (*rising; interrupting quickly*) Oh, a crested chaffinch! How interesting. (*To Chambert*) Oh, good morning; are you interested in birds?

CHAMBERT. I am not. I am only interested to see this apartment. (*To Nan*) Mrs Adams said it sounded ideal.

NAN. Si, si, si, signora.

CHAMBERT (*moving down* LC, *starting to examine the room*) I presume you do not mind if I look round?

NAN. No, no, no, signora.

CHAMBERT (*moving up* L *of the table to up* LC; *distastefully*) This is the drawing-room?

NAN. Si, si, si, signora.

CHAMBERT. The only drawing-room?

NAN. Si, si, si, signora.

CHAMBERT. Not very large, is it?

NAN. No, no, no, signora?

CHAMBERT. But then it is so crowded with furniture and bric-a-brac.

BEE (*moving to* R *of Chambert; indignantly*) Bric-a-brac!

NAN. Doris! Piano!

BEE (*moving to up* R *of the ottoman*) I don't like your treasures being called bric-a-brac, Contessa.

NAN. Enough, Doris. Depart. Presto! (*She waves her hand at Bee*)

(BEE *starts to leave the room*)

CHAMBERT (*taking no notice*) Of course it might look bigger if it were not for this wallpaper.

BEE (*stopping and turning; sharply*) What's the matter with the wallpaper? It's only been up five years, and I think . . .

ALICE (*rising and interrupting loudly*) A flock of seagulls! (*To Chambert*) A flock of seagulls in August. Most unusual. They should be at the seaside.

CHAMBERT. I am sure.

(ALICE *sits again*)

(*To Nan*) Where are the radiators?

(NAN *looks blank, then coughs into her handkerchief*)

NAN. Scusi.
CHAMBERT. I said, where are the radiators? (*Tapping her list*) It
says here that there is chauffage central.
BEE (*pointing to the cosy-stove*) This is the chauffage central.
CHAMBERT (*moving to the fireplace below the ottoman*) Chauffage
central! That out of date object?
BEE (*furious*) Let me tell you something . . .
ALICE (*rising and interrupting again*) Five wild ducks! Come and
look, madame.
CHAMBERT (*getting annoyed*) I have said: I am not interested.
(*To Nan*) There is constant hot water, I suppose?
NAN. Si, si, si, signora.
CHAMBERT. Worked by what system?

(NAN *coughs into her handkerchief*)

(*Moving to the double doors*) I should like to see the apparatus.

(NAN *coughs even more rackingly*)

(*Turning up* C) May the maid show me, please?
ALICE (*to Chambert*) The ducks are whirling round Albert's
Memorial. Most stirring.
CHAMBERT (*suspiciously; moving towards Alice*) There is something
odd here.
NAN. No, no, no, signora.
CHAMBERT. What is it? I come to inspect a modern luxury flat.
And what do I find? Something cramped and old-fashioned.
BEE. Cramped and old-fashioned! Before you say anything
more . . .
ALICE (*hastily to Nan*) Ring the bell—so that madame can see the
bedrooms.
NAN (*despairingly*) But the domestico is here.
ALICE. Never mind. Ring it!

(NAN *rings the handbell*)

NAN (*explaining to Chambert*) I ring for other domestico. She is less
stupido.

(*The door opens and a nervous* HATTIE *comes in with the folded stole*)

HATTIE. Oh! You have a visitor, Heloise.
NAN. Si. (*Introducing*) Madame Chambert.
HATTIE (*to Chambert*) Good morning. I just popped in because
I want my (*nodding towards Nan*) friend's advice. As she is French . . .
NAN (*quickly*) Italian.
HATTIE. Uum?
ALICE (*warningly*) You know the Contessa's Italian, dear.
HATTIE (*completely at sea*) Contessa?

NAN. Me! Do not be so stupido.

ALICE (*moving to* L *of Chambert*) It's Madame Chambert who's French, dear.

HATTIE. Oh. (*To Chambert*) You're the one who's French. (*Moving to* R *of Chambert*) Then it's you who can advise me . . . (*She starts unfolding the stole*)

CHAMBERT. I cannot. I am leaving. (*She crosses below Hattie towards the door*) I have been got here under false pretences, and I . . . (*She breaks off as she notices the fur which Hattie has unfolded. Her manner changes and she asks quite pleasantly*) Advise you about what, madame?

HATTIE. This mink stole. It came from Dior of Paris. I've been trying to sell it, and I can only . . .

CHAMBERT (*almost snatching it in her excitement*) You want to sell this Palomino?

ALICE. Her son's at a very expensive public school.

HATTIE (*explaining*) Yes, William.

CHAMBERT. How much do you want?

HATTIE. Well, I thought about a hundred and fifty pounds.

CHAMBERT (*obviously surprised*) A hundred and fifty?

HATTIE. Yes, but I suppose I might . . .

CHAMBERT (*interrupting*) I will give it to you.

(*They all gasp*)

BEE. You'll pay a hundred and fifty pounds for madame's fur?

(MADAME CHAMBERT, *carrying the fur, goes to the chair* L *of the table, sits, and takes a cheque-book from her handbag*)

CHAMBERT (*to Hattie*) I will give you a cheque for that amount immediately. (*She pauses, then asks hopefully*) Unless you have more furs you wish to dispose of?

HATTIE. No, I haven't.

NAN (*sharply; sitting up*) You would buy more, signora?

CHAMBERT. I would at least be interested to see them. (*She rises and moves down* C, *facing up stage*) I have a dress agency with branches in all the provinces; I am always looking for good nearly-new furs.

BEE (*excitedly*) You have a dress agency . . .

HATTIE. A permanent outlet!

(NAN *rises.* HATTIE *runs to* R *of the table. The* BRIGADIER, *wearing his monocle and pretending to be very bad-tempered, comes in with the bank statement and moves down* C)

BRIGADIER. Anyone seen that flipperty-jibbet wife of mine? (*Pretending to see Madame Chambert*) Oh, good morning.

CHAMBERT. Good morning.

BRIGADIER. Excuse me; I have urgent business with Henrietta.

BEE (*moving to* R *of the Brigadier and pulling his coat; pointedly*) The situation's rather changed, sir.

BRIGADIER. You'll change your job if you speak to me like that.

(BEE *moves to* L *of Nan down* RC)

(*To Hattie*) Just had me bank statement, Henrietta . . .
ALICE (*urgently*) It's not important, now . . .
BRIGADIER (*furiously*) Not important! (*Showing it*) Look at it—all in red! (*To Hattie*) You'll have to sell something, Henrietta.
NAN (*emphatically*) She has, signor! To this signora . . .
ALICE (*pointedly*) Who is looking for furs for her shops.
BRIGADIER (*slowly beginning to understand*) You want to buy furs?
BEE. Yes, she does, sir. Mightn't it be a chance to—help your wife's friends?

(ALICE *moves down* C *to* L *of Chambert*)

BRIGADIER (*slowly*) I see what you mean.
ALICE (*hurriedly explaining to Chambert*) When our friend discussed selling that stole, all sorts of people said they had furs, but didn't know how to get rid of them discreetly.
CHAMBERT. I should be only too willing to help.
HATTIE. Discreetly?
CHAMBERT. I am known for my discretion, madame.
ALICE. Would you mind if our friends did the sales through us?
CHAMBERT. Certainly not.
HATTIE (*excitedly moving to* R *of Chambert*) They don't like people knowing they're selling. Would you keep such transactions quite secret?
CHAMBERT. In my business it is not good to talk, madame.
BEE (*excitedly stepping in down* C) Having been with my ladies for so many years, I'm sure they won't mind my saying that the arrangements would be a little—eccentric.
CHAMBERT (*pointing to the Palomino*) If they get me such furs at such prices the arrangements can be quite mad!
NAN (*excitedly stepping in to* R *of Bee*) You would perhaps pay in pound notes?
CHAMBERT. If you wished.

(*The* BRIGADIER *brings the chair from* R *of the table to down* C. HATTIE *helps Chambert into it*)

BRIGADIER. Then sit down, Madame.

(MADAME CHAMBERT *sits*)

It looks as if we might have a most happy and profitable association.

(*They stand enthusiastically round her*)

Now; we don't want you to have the bother of coming here, so we'll always deliver the furs to you . . .
BEE. After dark, if that's suitable.

BRIGADIER. How many could you handle? (*He gets his clipboard from the table*)

NAN. Which do you prefer . . .

(*The* CURTAIN *starts to fall slowly*)

ALICE. Do you like mink?

HATTIE. Sable?

BEE. Ermine?

NAN. Chinchilla?

The CURTAIN *has fallen*

ACT III

SCENE—*The same. Six weeks later, evening.*

The curtains are drawn over the windows, the lights are on and the room looks attractive and comfortable. The table LC *is back in its original position, with two chairs above it and one to* R *of it. The stool is below it. The desk chair and armchair* LC *are back to their original positions.*

When the CURTAIN *rises,* ALICE, NAN *and* HATTIE *are seated at the table* LC, *which is piled high with pound notes.* ALICE *sits* R, HATTIE *up* R *and* NAN *up* L. ALICE *is counting out packets of notes,* HATTIE *placing them in large envelopes,* NAN *addressing the envelopes. All work with precision and method.*

ALICE. . . . ninety-four, ninety-five, ninety-six, ninety-seven, ninety-eight, ninety-nine, one hundred. (*Passing the bundle to Hattie*) Another hundred ready for Wrapping.

HATTIE (*passing her licked-up envelope to Nan*) Another hundred ready for Addressing. (*She takes Alice's notes, divides them into two, and places them in an envelope*)

NAN (*adding her addressed parcel to the pile on the table beside her*) Another hundred ready for Posting. (*She takes Hattie's envelope and starts addressing it*)

ALICE. Miraculous how business has improved since Madame Chambert's handled bulk sales.

HATTIE. Yes, we've done wonderfully the last six weeks. (*Suddenly anxious*) Though I'm sure she must be suspicious how we get the goods.

NAN. At the prices we let her have them she can't afford to be suspicious. (*Turning the page of her exercise book*) Hullo! That's the end of the addresses in the Notting Hill Gate area.

ALICE. Marvellous.

NAN. We shall soon be running out of "Deserving Cases".

ALICE. I can easily find more. I'll go and stay at some of the small hotels in the Cromwell Road.

HATTIE. Why the Cromwell Road specially?

ALICE. It's full of old ex-army people living on completely inadequate pensions.

HATTIE. Poor things. (*Pausing in her work*) Wonderful to think of their faces lighting up as they open these anonymous parcels.

NAN (*fervently*) Makes it all worth while.

ALICE (*happily*) Abundantly worth while. (*Passing notes to Hattie*) Another hundred ready for Wrapping.

HATTIE (*passing envelope to Nan*) Another hundred ready for Addressing.

NAN (*adding addressed parcel to the pile*) Another hundred ready for Posting.

HATTIE. That Posting pile's getting rather big. (*Rising*) I think I'll hide them away.

NAN. No hurry.

HATTIE (*sitting again*) I don't know why I feel so uneasy. I have, ever since I thought I saw that man in here last night.

ALICE (*patiently*) If someone had broken in, there'd be something missing, Hattie dear.

HATTIE. I was so frightened, I couldn't look properly; but I could have sworn he was over there—(*she points in the direction of the grandfather clock*) near the clock. And went out of the window when he saw me.

ALICE. There must be some odd drug in that nerve tonic of yours.

HATTIE. Perhaps I'd better stop taking it.

NAN. Not before the first of next month.

ALICE. No—we want you calm when we receive the cream of Harrods' "Mink Week".

(BEE *enters from the bedroom and crosses to* R *of Alice. She is resplendent in full evening dress, with a glittering ornament in her hair*)

BEE. All right?

ALICE. Bee, darling!

NAN. Smashing.

HATTIE. Lovely, Dame Beatrice.

BEE. If you look closely you can see why it was reduced. But fortunately the Albert Hall's not very well lit.

HATTIE. I'd have come if I'd known royalty was going to be there.

BEE. You're welcome to my seat, dear. I hate these charity performances.

ALICE. You're on the committee—you must suffer.

BEE (*waving her hand at the money*) But there's so much to be done here.

(*The* BRIGADIER *enters up* C *and moves down to the ottoman. He is very smart in old-fashioned evening dress and his medals*)

BRIGADIER. Damn laundry's shrunk my collar.

BEE. The effect is marvellous.

BRIGADIER. Hope this concert will be worth the agony, Beatrice.

BEE. I very much doubt it, but it's a wonderful charity—does immense good.

BRIGADIER (*looking at his watch*) Nearly three-quarters of an hour before we have to leave. We seem ready rather early.

BEE. If you'd had your way we'd have been ready at teatime. Let's help with money-parcelling for half an hour.

(*There is a long ring at the front-door bell*)

NAN. Probably Lily—I put the catch down.
ALICE. Ted may be with her.
BRIGADIER. Yes. First hiding-place.

(*They calmly and efficiently take up "cradle" positions.* NAN *and* ALICE *open the curtains.* HATTIE *and* BEE *take the cloth off the table with the money and money parcels in it*)

One.

(NAN *and* ALICE *let down the cradle*)

Two.

(HATTIE *and* BEE *put the cloth full of pound notes and parcels into the cradle*)

Three.

(NAN *and* ALICE *pull the cradle into position. The bell rings a series of rings*)

BEE (*calling*) All right, we've heard—coming.
ALICE. The sooner Ella Newcastle gets back from her holiday in Spain, the better.
HATTIE. Yes.
ALICE. Life's so much easier when Lily's safely there three hours a day.
BRIGADIER. Relax.

(*They settle about the room.* BEE *sits* R *on the ottoman, the* BRIGADIER *goes to the fireplace,* ALICE *sits in the armchair down* LC, HATTIE *sits up* R *of the table*)

Pass her in, Parry.

(NAN *opens the front door.* LILY *enters*)

LILY. 'Ere, what's the idea—locking me out?
NAN. Miss Hatfield thought she saw a strange man in the flat last night.
LILY (*moving down* C, *level with the ottoman; to Hattie*) Then was the time to lock the door—before he escaped you.
HATTIE. Lily!

(NAN *moves down to* L *of Hattie*)

BEE. Did they do your hair all right?
LILY. Yes. They've got a new bloke—he's a real dish!
ALICE. You've already got a dish. Concentrate on making him yours permanently, and leave other crockery alone.
LILY. Don't worry; if my new chiffon shift doesn't hook Ted at the Police Ball tomorrow, I retire from the Hunt.

HATTIE ⎫   ⎧ He'll propose.
NAN   ⎬ (*together*) ⎨ Of course.
BRIGADIER ⎪   ⎪ He'd better.
ALICE. ⎭   ⎩ He'll be very lucky.

BEE. I've ordered a new hat ready for the wedding.

LILY (*moved*) Thanks. That gives me more hope than even me new hair-do. (*She turns to go*)

ALICE (*over-casually*) By the way, when do you start again with Mrs Newcastle?

LILY (*sharply*) Why? What makes you ask?

ALICE (*surprised at her urgency*) She never said on the vulgar post-card she sent me.

LILY (*insistent*) You hadn't no special reason for finding out?

ALICE (*puzzled*) I just wondered when she was due back—that's all.

LILY. Monday week, then. Unless someone manages to push her into the bullring.

(LILY *exits*)

BRIGADIER. Why's she behaving like that?

BEE (*puzzled*) She's been odd the last day or two. I don't know what it is.

ALICE. Love.

HATTIE (*nervously; rising to* R *of Nan*) Perhaps she has a premonition that something's going to happen—as I have.

NAN. Fiddle-faddle. We're not expecting deliveries, and have nothing in the flat. What could happen?

(*In answer, the doorbell rings*)

HATTIE (*panic-stricken*) There! (*She moves to* L *of Nan*)

(ALICE *rises to the back of her armchair.* BEE *rises to the fireplace. The* BRIGADIER *tiptoes to the double doors to listen*)

BEE. Probably someone come to borrow something.

BRIGADIER. Nineteen hundred hours. A queer time for borrowing.

HATTIE (*moving to* L *of the double doors, working herself into hysteria*) I knew something was going to happen—I knew it! (*She switches off the lights*)

BRIGADIER. Hattie, please!

(HATTIE *switches on the lights again.* LILY *comes in, closing the door*)

LILY. The Irish have invaded again. (*Quizzically*) Do you want to see him, Dame dear?

BEE (*at a loss*) Well, er . . .

NAN. The poor beast wouldn't have come so late unless—(*weakly*) he had something interesting to tell us.

BEE (*after a moment*) Very well—show him in, Lily.

(LILY *shakes her head, displeased, and opens the door*)

LILY. You're to come in, Mr Hogan.

(MIKE *enters, trying to hide his nervous excitement*)

MIKE. That's most kind of you, me darlin'.

LILY. Don't you "darlin' " me, Leprechaun!

(LILY *exits*)

BRIGADIER (*angrily;* R *of Mike*) We laid down you were to telephone before coming here, Hogan.

MIKE. I'm desperate sorry to go against the regulations, General. But this is an emergency. (*Quickly covering that admittance*) At least, when I say it's an emergency, it's more that I could do you a good turn, only I got to do it quick.

ALICE (*sharply*) You've got some stuff?

MIKE (*moving down towards Alice*) A lovely little batch—you'll swoon.

(*They shoot questions at him*)

BRIGADIER (*moving down to* R *of him*) How many pieces?

MIKE. Six.

ALICE. Big or small?

MIKE. Mixed.

BEE. Mink?

MIKE. Mostly.

HATTIE. Quality?

MIKE. Stupendous—better than anything I've brought you before.

NAN. What's the hurry?

MIKE (*moving up stage*) There's no hurry, me darlin'! But it's getting towards nightfall, and . . .

BRIGADIER (*interrupting*) There's obviously an extreme hurry. The stuff's hot, isn't it?

MIKE (*coming down stage again*) No, no, no, not hot. A little warmish, perhaps. But perfectly safe. And fabulous!

ALICE. Why didn't you warn us you were bringing them?

MIKE (*despairingly*) I wasn't going to bring them. I was taking them to our old fence; it was a job planned before I knew you.

BRIGADIER. Why the change of plans?

MIKE (*ingratiatingly*) Well, when I saw the quality of the stuff, I thought of how you'd like it, so I said to me friends . . .

BEE (*interrupting*) You might as well tell us the truth, Mr Hogan. We always get it out of you in the end.

MIKE (*sitting on the stool below the table*) Dear Mother! Protect me from them. (*He rises*) All right. (*Resignedly*) It's a job that's gone wrong. The transport broke down. (*Pleading*) Now, be your sweet, clever, brave selves and . . .

BEE (*interrupting*) All right, stop the adjectives, and give us the details.

MIKE (*moving to below the ottoman to Bee*) Lady Beatrice, you're a doll. In my prayers I shall ask the blessed saints . . .

BRIGADIER (*moving down* C) Never mind the blessed saints! When are you bringing these furs?

MIKE. Pretty soon—if nothing's gone wrong while you've had me on the rack. (*He runs to the windows and peers out*)

(*The* BRIGADIER *follows to up* C, *watching him*)

HATTIE. No, no—we must have time to make preparations.

MIKE. Dear Mother, me friends are there. (*Hurrying into the room*) It's dangerous to leave them hovering. We'll be up immediately. (*He goes to the door*)

NAN (*moving up to* L *of Mike*) Wait a jiffy . . .

BRIGADIER. Yes, we must organize this properly.

MIKE. No time, General. Just ring and warn the hall porter that you're expecting us.

ALICE. But who are we expecting?

MIKE. Three musicians.

BEE. Three what?

MIKE. Musicians—(*gesturing*) scrape, scrape, peep, peep.

(MIKE *rushes out to the hall*)

NAN. Lily mustn't see them! (*Hurrying after him and shouting in a hoarse whisper*) Don't ring—tap gently.

MIKE. O.K.

(MIKE *runs out of the front door*)

HATTIE (*moving up to* L *of the doors*) What did he mean "scrape, scrape, peep, peep?"

BRIGADIER (*moving down* C; *in indecision*) He should have given us time to formulate a proper plan.

ALICE (*sitting on the stool below the table*) Well, he hasn't—so what do we do?

BEE (*moving up* R *of the ottoman; agitatedly*) You'd better telephone the hall porter, Nan.

(NAN *goes to the desk,* BEE *to the fireplace*)

NAN (*picking up the receiver and dialling*) To say what? What musicians?

BRIGADIER (*moving down* L) Probably better if you get him away from the hall altogether.

NAN. But how?

BRIGADIER (*at a loss*) Er—improvise.

NAN (*after a moment's thought; speaking into the phone in a very genteel Scots accent*) Hello? Hall porter? . . . Oh. I'm speaking for the lady in the top floor flat. She asked me to telephone because she can see

E

a person around at the back of the building. He's behaving—strangely. (*She listens*) Well, she didn't say exactly, but I gather something—unorthodox. (*She listens*) Will you? Straight away, before it gets more unorthodox? Thank you so much. (*She puts down the receiver*) O.K.

BRIGADIER. Good. (*He moves up* C) Now we must somehow anchor Lily to the kitchen.

BEE. One of us must go and chat to her . . .

(ALICE *rises and goes to Bee at the fireplace.* NAN *moves up* L)

ALICE. About Ted—love, marriage—that'll do it.

BEE. Right up your alley—off you go.

BRIGADIER. No, you and Alice must stay here to judge the furs.

ALICE. Nan must be on hand in case of phone calls.

BRIGADIER. Then it's you, Hatfield.

HATTIE (*appalled*) To talk to Lily about love?

BRIGADIER (*opening the doors for Hattie, to* R *of them*) Yes.

HATTIE. But I couldn't possibly! It's years since I've even—(*confused*) I mean, I haven't even—(*crying out*) I mean I couldn't possibly!

NAN (*pushing her out*) Of course you can. Think of that schoolteacher with the moustache.

HATTIE (*almost shrieking*) You promised never to tell anyone about him!

NAN. I haven't. But draw on that experience.

HATTIE. It's not fair. You make me feel like one of those women.

(NAN *gives her another push.* HATTIE *exits*)

BRIGADIER. This'll make us late for the concert.

BEE. It doesn't start for ages yet. And it's only a stone's throw away.

ALICE (*listening*) What's that?

(*They all listen. A gentle tapping on the front door is heard. They all panic slightly*)

NAN. They're here!

BRIGADIER. Now, no muddle. This is a time for order and system . . .

BEE (*moving up* C) It's not!

(*There is more tapping*)

If the tapping gets any louder Lily'll hear, however enthralling Hattie's experiences.

ALICE. Let them in, Nan.

(NAN *rushes out and opens the front door. They all watch anxiously. An unseen figure pushes something into Nan's arms and disappears, closing the front door.* NAN *staggers back in astonishment, and then comes into the room carrying two violin cases*)

NAN (*moving to* L *of the ottoman*) "Enter the first fiddles!"

(ALICE *moves* R *of the ottoman,* BEE *to above, the* BRIGADIER *to* L *of Nan*)

ALICE. The musicians! Quickly—open them, open them.

(NAN *puts them down and opens the first. They all exclaim in wonder as* BEE *takes out a beautiful mink jacket*)

BEE. An Emba "Autumn Haze" mink jacket.
ALICE. This season's model, I'd say.
NAN. It's a smasher.
BRIGADIER. First rate. Madame Chambert was asking for more short mink.
BEE (*taking the empty case to the stool* LC) The other. What's in the other?

(NAN *opens the other case. Again all exclaim in wonder*)

NAN. Great Scott!
ALICE (*taking it out*) It's even better than the first.
BRIGADIER. What is it, Beatrice?
BEE (*taking it*) Very rare. Empress Chinchilla.
ALICE. Unbelievably expensive.
NAN. More expensive than mink?
ALICE. Heavens, yes.

(*Tapping is heard again. The* BRIGADIER *takes the case from the stool*)

They're here again!
BRIGADIER. We'd better replace these.
ALICE. Yes. (*She starts to replace them in the cases*)
BEE. No! It just might be someone on their trail. They'd expect them to be in the cases. Let's hide them in the ottoman—just for the meantime. (*She takes both jackets*)
BRIGADIER. Agreed. (*He takes the second case. Ordering*) Sofa drill!

(NAN *and* ALICE *open the ottoman.* BEE *goes below it*)

Action!

(NAN *and* ALICE *bend over and open the ottoman.* BEE *deftly places the furs inside.* ALICE *and* NAN *close the ottoman. Louder tapping is heard*)

Door, Parry.

(NAN *takes the violin cases and goes to the front door. The* BRIGADIER *follows up to* L *of the doors,* BEE *to* R. ALICE *stands* R *of the ottoman.* NAN *opens the front door. An unseen figure deposits two french horn cases on the floor.* NAN *pushes her cases into his arms. He disappears, closing the front door.* NAN *staggers to* L *of the ottoman with the new cases, followed by the* BRIGADIER *to her* L *and* BEE *above it*)

NAN. Coming in with the brass.

BEE. I've always loved the french horn. I think I'm going to like it even more.

BRIGADIER. Disclose!

(NAN *opens a horn case and draws out a large mink stole. Again all exclaim in delight*)

BEE. A stole of finest Tourmaline mink.

ALICE. It's quite magnificent.

BRIGADIER (*taking the case to the stool*) Most saleable.

NAN. So long! Perhaps we could cut it and sell it as two?

BEE. Isn't this exciting? Just like Christmas.

(NAN *opens the second case and takes out a white fox creation*)

BEE. It's so lovely I daren't touch it.

ALICE (*taking it*) I dare!

BRIGADIER. Mink?

BEE. No. Glorious white arctic fox.

ALICE. Coming back into fashion. It'll soon be as expensive as mink.

NAN. There's another at the bottom! (*She takes out another mink stole*)

BRIGADIER. Not as showy as the others.

BEE. But equally expensive—Black Diamond mink.

ALICE. Terribly chic.

NAN. It means we'll be able to start distributing money parcels in the Hammersmith area.

(*More tapping*)

BEE (*excitedly*) More!

BRIGADIER. Positions!

(*They take up their positions at the ottoman as before*)

Action!

(*They hide the furs as before. Louder tapping*)

NAN (*rushing out*) Coming!

(*The BRIGADIER follows to L of the double doors, BEE and ALICE to R of them. They all peer excitedly as she opens the front door. This time MIKE staggers in carrying a tuba case. NAN closes the front door. MIKE goes to below the chair R of the table, ALICE and BEE to R of him, NAN and the BRIGADIER to up L of him*)

MIKE. Other members of me band arrive all right?

BEE. Yes, and we think we'll be able to have quite a good concert.

MIKE. Wait till you hear the tuba.

BEE. We can't wait.

ALICE. Show us, show us.

MIKE. What I have here is a symphony in itself. (*He opens the case and slowly draws out a full-length coat*)

BEE (*in a hushed voice*) A full-length coat of superb Dawn Pastel mink.

ALICE. It's dreamy!

BEE. Mr Hogan, dear, we forgive you all the pain and anguish you've caused us. (*She takes the coat and arranges it over the armchair*)

MIKE (*backing away below the ottoman*) She's a beauty, isn't she?

ALICE (*in ecstasy*) She's every woman's hope realized, Mr Hogan.

(HATTIE *enters*)

HATTIE (*exclaiming in wonder*) Oh, how lovely.

ALICE. Isn't it gorgeous?

BRIGADIER (*anxiously*) What about Lily?

HATTIE. Safely doing her football pools. (*She circles the armchair to down* L *of it, then closes in to the armchair and strokes the fur*) It's as beautiful as autumn leaves.

(*They all crowd round, murmuring with pleasure,* BEE *to* R *of the chair,* ALICE *up* L *of her,* NAN L *of the chair,* HATTIE *down* L)

NAN. Excellent condition.

ALICE. It's a preview of Paradise.

BEE. The fur flows like a deep river.

BRIGADIER (*crossing below Mike to the fireplace*) Extraordinary what a bit of fur can do to a woman. We'll discuss prices tomorrow.

MIKE. Tomorrow it shall be, General. I'll get off and check me alibis. I'll ring you later. (*He turns up* C)

BRIGADIER. Not tonight. We're off to this charity do at the Albert Hall.

MIKE (*returning and flopping on the ottoman* L) You're not! Dear Mother! (*He bursts into laughter*)

BEE (*moving to him*) What's so amusing?

MIKE. Just that you're not going to get your money's worth.

BRIGADIER. Why not?

MIKE. You know how the programme's supposed to end?

BEE. Certainly, I'm on the committee. Six specially chosen débutantes are going to show . . . (*She breaks off with a slight scream*) Don't say these are the furs they were going to model!

MIKE. You're right as usual, Lady Beatrice.

BEE (*turning on him*) You fool! You silly, damn, silly damn fool!

MIKE (*rising*) Here, what's this now?

BEE. That concert's in aid of our favourite charity!

(ALICE *moves to* L *of Bee,* HATTIE *to* L *of Nan*)

ALICE. Now they'll be sued by the firm who lent the furs, and lose thousands.

BRIGADIER. It's monstrous. Something must be done. And immediately. (*Moving to Mike and speaking urgently*) Tell us exactly how you took the furs.
MIKE. I will not.
BRIGADIER. You will.
ALL. Yes!

(*The* BRIGADIER, BEE *and* ALICE *move to the double doors, barring his way*)

MIKE (*apprehensively*) Here, here, what are you up to?
ALICE (*significantly*) If you don't talk, we ring up your wife and tell her about Beryl.
MIKE (*quickly*) I don't know anyone called Beryl!
BRIGADIER. No? The evidence, Parry.

(NAN *hurries to the bookshelves down* L *and takes out a book, from which she removes two snapshots*)

Miss Parry's camera is old, but very efficient.

(NAN *moves down* LC *and holds out the snaps*)

MIKE (*horrified*) No-one would believe it!
ALICE (*moving down to* L *of Mike*) I think they would. You both come out very well.
MIKE. I mean that such an innocent-looking bunch would go to such lengths. (*Resignedly*) All right. I'll tell.

(NAN *returns the snaps to the book and the book to the shelves. She then comes behind the armchair* LC)

BRIGADIER. Quickly and concisely.

(MIKE *sits on the ottoman,* L *end. The* BRIGADIER *stands up* L *of him,* BEE *to* R *of the Brigadier,* ALICE *down* C, HATTIE LC)

MIKE. Well, after the dress-rehearsal this afternoon, the furs were locked in dressing-room forty-four.
BRIGADIER. Forty-four.
MIKE. The two security guards then took up their position in the room opposite.
BEE. Yes?
MIKE. One of my girls had "cultivated" the younger guard and got employed in the opera scene. She took a bottle of Scotch along to the two men.
NAN. Drugged?
MIKE (*nodding*) When they were out cold, she took the key and let us into forty-four. We nicked the stuff, relocked, and would now be on our way to Liverpool except for a broken fuel-pump.
BRIGADIER. Instead?
MIKE. We saw the instrument cases and used them to smuggle the stuff here.

ALICE. Will the loss have been discovered?

MIKE. Doubtful. The debutantes don't appear till the end of the programme and have been told to keep out of the way till the interval.

BEE. Where's the key now?

MIKE. Probably back on the guard.

BRIGADIER. Are they still unconscious?

MIKE. My guess would be till midnight.

BEE (*efficiently brisk*) All right. Now, get out.

MIKE. Eh?

ALICE. You're free to hurry off to Beryl.

MIKE (*worriedly; rising*) I don't like the sound of all this. Why have you put me through this Inquisition?

HATTIE (*moving to L of Mike and suddenly confronting him with surprising energy*) You talk about the Inquisition! You who go round drugging people and playing fast and loose behind your poor wife's back . . .

NAN. Hattie . . .

HATTIE (*taking no notice*) Your conduct appals me, Mr Hogan. So much so that I feel—muddled—fuddled—oh . . . (*She faints against the alarmed Mike*)

BRIGADIER. No, no, Hatfield.

BEE. It's no use saying "no, no"; she has. Put her on the ottoman.

(*The* BRIGADIER *takes Hattie's shoulders,* MIKE *her feet, and they put her on the ottoman.* ALICE *kneels below it, patting her hands. The* BRIGADIER *gets a paper from the canterbury and starts fanning her*)

BRIGADIER. Now be off, before you do any more harm.

MIKE. But I didn't do anything! I can't leave—not knowing what you're up to.

NAN (*moving towards the phone*) Your home telephone number's Wimbledon seven-two-double-three, isn't it?

MIKE (*moving to the door*) Dear Mother, you know even that! All right, I'm going.

BEE. Here! (*Pointing to the cases*) Take your empties!

MIKE. To think I left home this morning a happy, confident man. (*Shaking his head*) Still, I suppose I must thank the blessed saints you haven't drained off me blood. (*He puts the smaller cases into the large one*)

(MIKE *staggers out with the cases*)

BEE. You realize what we've got to do?

(ALICE *rises, to down* C)

BRIGADIER. Replace the furs, of course.

NAN. The charity'll be ruined otherwise.

ALICE. The room where they should be is locked—how are we going to get in?

HATTIE (*sitting up*) With the key. (*She holds one up*) I think this is it. (*Looking*) Yes—forty-four.

(*The* BRIGADIER *takes the key*)

NAN. Hattie!

HATTIE. I felt in my bones he really had it, so I thought I'd faint and find out.

NAN. Clever beast!

BRIGADIER. We've let him take the containers! What are we going to return the furs in?

BEE (*after a moment's thought*) Not "in" anything. "On" our backs. It'll be a smart audience—we'll mingle in, wearing them.

BRIGADIER. I'm not wearing any fur!

BEE (*moving to Alice*) Alice, go and slip on my other evening dress.

ALICE. That old thing!

BEE. I met Queen Mary in it. If it was good enough for her, it's good enough for you. (*She pushes Alice above the armchair*) Go along.

ALICE. And I have such a divine unworn frock hanging up in the hotel!

(BEE *pushes* ALICE *off down* L. *She returns to* L *of Nan*)

BRIGADIER (*circling the ottoman to up* C) The plan forms. You and Alice go into the hall on the two tickets, wearing the first two furs—make your way back stage . . .

BEE (*nodding*) As a member of the Committee, no-one will question.

BRIGADIER. Find room forty-four, unlock it, replace the furs, then back here at the double.

BEE. Then collect two more and repeat the action.

NAN. Won't it look odd you going in and out three times wearing different furs?

BEE (*worried*) Oh, yes. It will. Especially when they've only seen me in my old "Mothy" before.

BRIGADIER (*to Nan and Hattie*) You two must take your turns.

HATTIE (*rising to the fireplace*) Oh, no, I couldn't! I haven't even got an evening dress.

NAN (*to* L *of Hattie*) Yes, yes; I'll botch up something for you.

HATTIE (*apprehensively*) Oh dear, will you?

NAN. I have a mass of stage stuff. Including jewellery. With a few rings and necklaces . . .

BRIGADIER (*roaring*) This isn't a fashion show! Prepare!

(NAN *and* HATTIE *rush out of the double doors*)

(*Looking at his watch*) Nineteen-ten hours. See if the audience is arriving, Beatrice.

BEE (*going to the window*) Yes. Not many—but enough to get lost in.

BRIGADIER (*going to the bedroom door*) Then you'd better lead off your patrol. (*Banging on the door*) Miller! On parade! (*He returns to down* C)

(ALICE *enters to below the armchair. She wears a rather ornate evening dress and carries long white gloves*)

ALICE. I'm not even zipped up yet. (*To Bee, presenting her back*) Here.

(BEE *goes to* R *of Alice and operates*)

I don't care if these are your best gloves—(*putting them on*) I had to have something belonging to this century.
BRIGADIER. You look splendid. (*Opening the ottoman*) Now: don equipment. Which coats are you starting off with?

(ALICE, L *of the armchair, and* BEE, R *of it, both grab the full-length coat*)

ALICE }
BEE } (*together*) This one!
BRIGADIER. You can't both wear it!
ALICE. Toss a coin, Bertie. (*To Bee*) Heads you wear it; tails I do.

(*The* BRIGADIER *flicks a coin*)

Well?
BRIGADIER. Heads.
BEE. Sorry, darling. (*She starts to put on the coat*)
BRIGADIER (*taking the chinchilla from the ottoman*) What about this chap, Alice?
ALICE (*going to* L *of him*) Yes, quickly—before I have to toss with the others.

(*The* BRIGADIER *helps her into the fur*)

BEE (*slipping out of the coat*) No, I won't wear it. It's too selfish. It would give Hattie the thrill of her life.
BRIGADIER (*irritated*) Well, make up your mind, for Heaven's sake!

(BEE *leaves the coat on the armchair, goes to the ottoman, takes out the Tourmaline stole, puts it on, and closes the ottoman*)

BEE. I'll make do with the Tourmaline.

(ALICE *moves* L *of her* BEE *and* ALICE *admire each other excitedly*)
ALICE. Darling, you look like a million dollars.

(*The* BRIGADIER, *exasperated, moves away down* LC)

Bee. So do you! That colour brings out the highlights in your hair.
Alice. Yours makes your skin look like cream.
Bee. Yours has the effect . . .
Brigadier (*roaring*) Stop luxuriating! Get ready to move off.
Bee (*crossing below Alice to* c) Sorry, Bertie.
Brigadier. Second issue of equipment. Appleby! (*He gives the key and tickets to Bee*) The key of room forty-four. And the concert tickets. Any questions?
Alice. No, I have my smelling salts in case we need perking up.
Brigadier (*very seriously*) Then let me warn you. This expedition is dangerous, very dangerous. Slip up, and *we'll* be accused of the theft.
Alice. Oh, no.
Brigadier. That could mean the showing up of our whole organization.
Bee. You'll have me deserting in a moment.
Alice. Have I time for a tiny whisky?
Brigadier. No! (*Counting as he looks at his watch*) Ready? Five, four, three, two, one—Action!

(Alice *and* Bee *fly to the front door and go out. The* Brigadier *jots down the timing on his cuff and then goes to watch at the window*)

Nan (*off*) Come on, Hattie—buck up!

(Nan *enters and goes above the ottoman for a cigarette from the table. She is strangely dressed in evening dress. The* Brigadier *watches in amazement as she lights the cigarette*)

Brigadier. Striking.
Nan. What?
Brigadier. The kit.
Nan (*drily*) Thanks. The first patrol's gone?
Brigadier (*studying his watch*) If the lift was free they should be emerging any moment. Take over guard.

(Nan *goes to the window. He moves away to up* lc)

Nan. No sign yet.
Brigadier. Where on earth's Hatfield? (*Shouting*) Hatfield!
Hattie (*off*) Coming.

(Hattie *enters, looking odd in a too long dress and much theatrical jewellery*)

(*Closing the doors*) How do I look?
Brigadier. Er—very—effective.
Nan. Jolly good.
Hattie. There's still more jewellery in the box. Shall I . . . ?
Brigadier (*hastily*) No, no!
Nan (*at the window*) There they are now!

(Hattie *and the* Brigadier *hurry to the window*)

BRIGADIER (*jotting it down on his cuff*) Thirty-five seconds.
HATTIE. Where?
NAN. There. Those two weaving in and out like snow leopards.
HATTIE. Oh, yes. (*Nervously*) Oh dear, I do hope everything will go all right.
NAN. They've entered the Hall.
BRIGADIER. Forty-eight seconds. (*Moving up* C) You two had better prepare in case of emergency.
HATTIE. Don't say it—you may attract it!
BRIGADIER. Beatrice suggested the coat for Hatfield.
HATTIE (*delighted*) Oh, how lovely!

(*The* BRIGADIER *returns to the window.* HATTIE *goes to the armchair, puts on the coat slowly in silence. Then she stands, rocking slightly on her feet, eyes closed, in complete bliss*)

Next life I'm going to earn one of these.
BRIGADIER. Come along, come along! I'll relieve you at your post, Parry.
HATTIE. Which are you going to have? (*She hurries to the ottoman*)

(NAN *goes to* L *of the ottoman. Together they open it*)

NAN. Let's see what's left. (*She takes out an armful of furs*)

(HATTIE *closes the ottoman and they lay the furs out on top*)

BRIGADIER (*watching the street*) I should take the next biggest of the three left.
NAN (*puzzled*) Three? There are four.
BRIGADIER. Nonsense.
HATTIE. It's true, Brigadier.
BRIGADIER (*dogmatically*) Hogan delivered six. Beatrice has taken one; Alice one. Hattie's got one on. That leaves three.
NAN. There are four. (*Holding them up in turn*) One, two, three, four.
BRIGADIER. Impossible! (*He hurries to the ottoman and counts*) One, two, three—four. (*Amazed*) There are four.
NAN. I've kept telling you.
BRIGADIER. Then one's an interloper.
NAN. But how's it got amongst ours?
HATTIE. It must have already been in the ottoman when you put the others in.
BRIGADIER. But we haven't used the ottoman since Lily had the hinge done. Which is it?
NAN (*searching*) We oughtn't to have sent both the experts off at once. (*Picking up a white fur cape*) But I'd bet on this.
BRIGADIER. Why?
HATTIE. It doesn't seem as good as the others.
BRIGADIER. Then that's the nigger in the woodpile.

HATTIE. Are we going to return it with the rest of the wood-pile?

BRIGADIER. Well . . .

(*Before he can answer, there is a loud ringing at the front door.* HATTIE *starts to scream, but the* BRIGADIER *claps his hand over her mouth*)

BRIGADIER (*in a whisper*) It can't be Alice and Beatrice back.

HATTIE. It's the police—it's the police! (*She runs to below* NAN *at the fireplace*)

NAN (*smacking her quite hard*) Shh!

BRIGADIER. Emergency Storage!

(*In her panic* HATTIE *has difficulty getting out of her coat, but they eventually replace the furs in the ottoman*)

Operation Relaxation!

(NAN *lies on the ottoman,* HATTIE *blows dust off vases on the mantel-piece, the* BRIGADIER *sits below the fire reading "The Times".*
The door opens and a perturbed LILY *enters*)

LILY. It's Ted. Says he must see you. I've tried to . . .

(TED, *in uniform, hurries in to down* C)

TED. Sorry to burst in, but it's urgent. And I can't stay more than a mo'.

BRIGADIER. Yes?

TED. I thought I better warn you—in case you get a fright.

NAN. About what?

TED. It's obviously a mistake of some sort. But I was on telephone duty at the station just now, and an old bird rang up in such a state that I couldn't make out exactly what she was at. But it seems she came back unexpected from holiday, to find her best fur gone. Then she gave this address . . .

LILY (*distraught; moving above the ottoman*) This address!

TED. And said we should send someone round quick.

BRIGADIER. It's absurd.

TED. Yes, I'm sure there's nothing to it, but I thought I better prepare you. A detective inspector's gone round to see the old girl and'll then come straight on here.

HATTIE. Here!

TED (*going to the door*) If I'm caught off duty it'll be the end of my job.

LILY (*following him up* C) One moment, Ted . . .

TED (*taking Lily's arm*) I daren't. Come with me to my bike—I'll explain more.

LILY. No, Ted . . .

TED. Come on—or I may be seen.

(TED *hurries the unhappy* LILY *off with him, and the front door slams.* HATTIE, NAN *and the* BRIGADIER *spring to life*)

HATTIE (*running up and down* C) This is terrible!

(*The* BRIGADIER *rises*)

NAN. It's murder.

HATTIE. What are we going to do—what are we going to do?

BRIGADIER (*moving up and down* R) Trust me. I'm thinking. The situation's vital. Observe, Parry.

(NAN *hurries to the window. The* BRIGADIER *paces* R)

HATTIE (*frantically*) The Inspector may be here before Dame Beatrice and Alice get back.

NAN. No sign of them.

HATTIE (*to up* LC) And there's that ottoman stuffed with hot furs.

BRIGADIER (*to up* C) We must alter plans. You two must leave immediately, trusting to meet the others en route.

HATTIE. But there are only two of us and all those furs!

BRIGADIER. You must somehow carry the extras.

NAN (*hurrying to the ottoman*) You could wear the jacket under the coat, Hattie.

HATTIE (*to* L *of her*) Oh, yes. And perhaps the stole round my middle as before.

NAN. You'd look like a breeding polar bear. I'll wear it.

(NAN *opens the ottoman and takes out the furs*)

HATTIE. What about the interloper?

NAN (*throwing the ermine cape into the armchair down* R) No time to bother about that. (*Going to the Brigadier* C) Here, help me, Brigadier.

(*The* BRIGADIER *holds the smaller stole for her while she twists so that it is wound round her waist.* HATTIE *puts on the jacket and then the fur coat over it. The* BRIGADIER *dashes to the window*)

HATTIE (*going to* R *of Nan*) I'm cold with fright even under all this.

BRIGADIER. If only I could see Beatrice.

NAN (*moving towards the table* LC) If only you don't see a police car.

HATTIE (*running to the doors*) Oh don't!

NAN (*catching her*) Where are you going?

HATTIE. Nerve tonic.

NAN. No. We don't want you seeing more strange men all over the place. (*She goes to the ottoman*) Help me with this coat.

(HATTIE *goes to* L *of Nan to help her*)

BRIGADIER. Hasten, hasten! Are you ready?

NAN. All correct.

(*They stand together huddled in furs*)

BRIGADIER (*moving to* L *of them*) Prepare to leave immediately.
NAN. Inspect us to make sure nothing's hanging out.

(*The* BRIGADIER *marches round them as in a military inspection*)

BRIGADIER. All correct. Action!

(HATTIE *and* NAN *hold the furs round them and rush out of the front door, through which* LILY *enters at the same moment*)

LILY (*very agitatedly, to up* C) What's that they've got on?
BRIGADIER. They're returning some furs that were left by mistake.
LILY (*frantically*) Not the one I took?
BRIGADIER. Um?
LILY. Mrs Newcastle's fur.
BRIGADIER. What! (*Hurrying down* R *and picking up the fur*) This is Mrs Newcastle's fur?
LILY (*moving down* RC *and taking the fur*) I borrowed it for the Police Ball tomorrow—so I'd put that bloody Shirley in the shade. I thought Mrs N. was away for another week. (*Moving down* L) Oh, what are we going to do?
BRIGADIER. I'll think of something.
LILY. Quickly, then. Or the Inspector will be here, and then . . .

(BEE *and* ALICE *enter breathlessly through the front door.* BEE *moves down* LC, ALICE *to above the ottoman*)

BEE. Done!
BRIGADIER. Satisfactorily?
BEE. Well, we got them back.
BRIGADIER. Did you meet the others?
ALICE. Yes, and gave them the key and tickets.
BEE. What's all this about a detective?
LILY (*showing it*) He's coming about Mrs Newcastle's fur which I took.
BEE. Really, Lily, you are tiresome.
ALICE. We must just say you borrowed it.
LILY. But Mrs N.'s reported it as stolen! If they discover it here they'll make enquiries—find out I've been in Holloway—and Ted'll leave me, I know he will!
BEE (*firmly*) We can't have that. We must hide it.
LILY. But where?

(*The front-door bell rings*)

My Gawd! The Inspector!

(*Everyone panics and moves about distractedly*)

BRIGADIER (*bustling about aimlessly with the others*) Now, keep calm, keep calm, keep calm!

BEE. Quick, Lily, the fur! (*She grabs the fur from Lily, puts it in the ottoman, and lies on it*)

(*The* BRIGADIER *goes up to the doors.* ALICE *gets the embroidery bag and gives it to Bee*)

(*To Lily*) Don't worry—we'll see you through. Let him in.

LILY. I daren't!

BRIGADIER (*coming down to Lily and slapping her on the behind*) Get along at once. And look cheerful.

(LILY *puts on a sickly smile and, going into the hall, closes the doors as the bell rings again*)

ALICE (*in a frantic whisper; going to the Brigadier* C) This is too awful! If he finds the fur, it'll make him suspicious, and he'll search further. Think of all the money parcels up there!

BEE. Don't worry, he won't find the fur. He's not going to get me off this.

BRIGADIER (*settling below the fire with "The Times"*) If he's a good one he will.

BEE. I'm a Dame of the British Empire. I'll behave as it sounds for once.

(ALICE *hears the doors opening, rushes to the desk, takes the flowers out of the vase on it, and starts to put them in again.* LILY *enters.* BEE *puts on her grandest manner*)

BEE (*loudly*) "There's a perfectly easy solution," I said: "bring back flogging."

LILY. Detective Inspector Wilson to see you, Dame dear.

BEE. Show him in.

(*A pleasant, rather pretty woman of about thirty, plainly dressed in civilian clothes, comes in*)

WILSON. Good evening.

(*They all turn*)

BEE. Who's this? I said show the Inspector in.

WILSON. I am the Inspector.

(LILY *closes the doors and stands* L. *The* BRIGADIER *rises, leaving the newspaper in the armchair*)

BEE (*momentarily nonplussed*) Oh? Odd.

WILSON (*smiling*) Not really, we don't always go about in uniform. (*Moving down* C) I'm sorry to disturb you, madam; but I've just been round to see a Mrs Newcastle. She accuses your maid Lily of having stolen a valuable fur.

BEE. Ella wouldn't know a valuable fur from a diseased rabbit.

WILSON. She describes it as a white ermine jacket.

BEE. And what gives the old idiot the idea that my maid purloined it?

WILSON. I gather she works there and is the only one with keys to the flat. There was no sign of breaking in.

BRIGADIER (*very blimpish; sitting again*) Expect she pawned it, and forgot.

BEE. Yes. (*Very indignantly*) I take this as a personal affront, Inspector. And I promise you—heads shall fall!

WILSON (*patiently*) Would you have any objection to my searching Lily's room?

BEE. If you do I shall write to the Prime Minister. But carry on.

WILSON. Thank you, madam. (*To Lily*) Show me where it is.

(*As* LILY *opens the door,* NAN *and* HATTIE *dash in.* NAN *goes down level with the chair* R *of the table* LC, HATTIE *up* R *of her*)

NAN. He hasn't come yet? (*Seeing Wilson*) Oh!

ALICE (*loudly*) No, he rang and said his Daimler had broken down and we were to start dinner without him.

BEE. Show the Detective Inspector what she wants, Lily.

(HATTIE *staggers on hearing the name*)

WILSON. Thank you.

(WILSON *and* LILY *exit. The* BRIGADIER *rises*)

NAN (*in a whisper*) That's him?

BEE. Yes, and she's come about the fur in here that Lily pinched.

NAN (*sitting on the stool* LC) Christmas!

HATTIE. It's too much on top of what we've just been through.

BRIGADIER. But you got your lot back all right?

(*They nod*)

Then all forces concentrate on this danger point.

BEE (*rising*) I'm not happy. We won't be able to get round her as we would a man.

ALICE. No. (*Pointing*) And it's shrieking to be found in a conspicuous place like that.

BRIGADIER. Keep watch at the door, Hatfield.

(HATTIE *flies to the doors and peers through the keyhole*)

BEE (*taking the fur out of the ottoman*) Where would be safer?

(*They all search round the room.* BEE *works her way from fireplace to window. The* BRIGADIER *crosses to down* C. NAN *rises to up* C, ALICE *works to up* L. *They all look for a hiding-place*)

NAN. What about the cosy-stove?

ALICE. First place I should look.

NAN (*acidly*) Well, where's the last?

ALICE. The grandfather clock?

BRIGADIER. Obvious place to hide something.

HATTIE. Say you took a bath, made the water soapy, and put the fur in with you?

BEE (*up* C, *to* L *of Hattie*) I'd never take a bath while she's here!

BRIGADIER. Shall we just throw it out of the window?

ALICE. She'll have come in a police car—the driver might see it floating down.

BEE (*pointing to the window*) Could we put it in the cradle instead of the money?

ALICE. If she finds hundreds of pounds lying about we'll all be in Holloway for sure.

HATTIE. Oh, don't!

NAN (*to down* C) Bingo! Got it! She'll never look in small places. We must cut it up and hide the bits in vases. (*She goes to the fireplace*)

ALICE. Oh, no, it'd be sacrilege.

BRIGADIER (*going to the embroidery bag on the ottoman for the scissors*) It's a solution. Scissors, quickly!

ALICE (*sitting in the armchair down* LC) I'd rather go to jail.

NAN. You will, if we don't.

HATTIE. Oh!

BRIGADIER (*giving the scissors to Bee*) You're the expert.

(BEE *moves down* C, *takes the scissors, poises them, then lowers them*)

BEE. It's no good, Alice is right. It's too lovely.

BRIGADIER (*furiously*) You women! Here, give them to me. (*He seizes the fur and the scissors*)

HATTIE (*at the keyhole*) They're coming back!

(NAN *picks up the newspaper from the armchair down* R *and swats flies on the mantelpiece.* BEE *seizes the fur from the Brigadier, throws it in the ottoman, and lies down as before.* HATTIE *goes into the window bay and draws the window curtains. The* BRIGADIER *takes another paper from the canterbury and sits down* R.

LILY *enters with* WILSON *and stands* L *of the doors.* WILSON *comes down to* L *of the ottoman*)

BEE (*booming again*) Did you locate the loot?

WILSON (*smilingly*) No, madam.

BEE. Then: good night, Inspectress.

WILSON. I wonder if you'd mind answering a few questions before I go?

NAN (*abruptly*) Are we all to be grilled?

WILSON. No, madam.

NAN. Then you will excuse me. I have an elocution pupil waiting for her lesson. (*She goes up* C)

WILSON (*moving up to* L *of her*) Just a moment, madam. I think it would perhaps be better . . .

NAN (*severely*) You could do with a lesson or two yourself. Your final consonants are very shaky. (*Crisply quoting, emphasizing the final consonants*):

F

Hark to the mingled din
Of fife, and steed, and trump, and drum,
And roaring culverin.

(NAN *has left the room before the amazed* WILSON *can recover*)

ALICE. You must excuse her, Inspector; she's a little blunt.
WILSON. I like plain speaking.
BRIGADIER (*irritably; rising*) Then I'll give you some, madam. I consider that to march in here . . .
WILSON (*charmingly interrupting him, moving down* C) I'm only too anxious to march out again, sir. So perhaps you'll let me get on. (*Looking round speculatively*) There's a possibility that the fur may be hidden in here. May I have a quick look, madam?
BEE. Break so much as a (*emphasizing final consonants*) match stick, and I'll sue.
WILSON. I won't disturb anything. (*Quite unostentatiously, she circles from down* C *to* L *then up to the window, searching or feeling in any possible hiding-place. She goes on speaking while doing this. Among other places, she glances in the grandfather clock*)
BEE. Just as I shall sue that wicked Newcastle woman for slander or libel, whichever it is.

(WILSON *opens the curtains and discovers* HATTIE *watering flowers*)

HATTIE. Good evening.
WILSON (*continuing to* L *of Lily*) Lily tells me she's been with you for five years. Do you agree?

(*They are all watching the search with great anxiety while pretending not to be interested*)

BEE. Well, let me see. She came to me on the day I was first invited to luncheon at Buckingham Palace . . .
LILY. It is five years—I can show you my cards.
WILSON (*coming down* C) And how long has she been with Mrs Newcastle?

(HATTIE *comes to* R *of the table*)

BEE. I can tell you how long she'll stay after this.

(WILSON *stops her move round the room and looks at the ottoman*)

WILSON. Does the ottoman open, madam?
BEE (*too alarmed to utter*) Uuuuum?
WILSON. It looks as if there's a container in that piece you're lying on. May I look?

(*There is an awful pause, which is punctured by a drawn-out moan from* HATTIE, *who comes* C *and slides to the floor in a dead faint*)

ALICE (*moving above the armchair* LC) Hattie! She's fainted, the poor dear.

BRIGADIER (*moving to* C) Quickly, Inspector—help me.

(*The* BRIGADIER *takes Hattie's shoulders,* WILSON *takes her feet*)

ALICE (*to Wilson*) She thought she saw a burglar in here last night and has been nervy ever since.
BEE (*rising from the ottoman*) Put her on here.
WILSON. No, this will do.

(*There is a tug-of-war with Hattie's body. But* WILSON *wins, and* HATTIE *is deposited in the armchair* LC, *where she lies practically unseen*)

WILSON (*to Lily*) Give her some water.

(LILY *turns to exit.* WILSON *turns her back on Hattie and concentrates on* BEE, *who has taken the opportunity to lie on the ottoman again*)

WILSON. May I look in the ottoman, madam?

(LILY *stops.* WILSON *moves to* L *of the ottoman*)

BEE (*desperately playing for time*) This ottoman?
WILSON. Yes.
BEE. Well—(*faintly, in despair*) I can't think why not. (*She rises*)

(WILSON'S *hand goes out to lift the lid. The telephone rings.* BEE *takes the opportunity to sit again*)

Oh, that bell! It always gives me such a fright. Answer it, Alice dear, will you? I don't hear so well, Inspector.
ALICE (*answering the phone*) Yes? . . . Yes . . . Who? . . . Oh, yes. Just hold on, will you? (*Covering the receiver*) It's for you, Inspector.
WILSON. Me?
ALICE. They're asking for the Detective Inspector who's here.
WILSON. Thank you. (*She takes the receiver*) Yes? (*She listens*) Oh, yes. (*She listens and is obviously displeased*) When? (*She listens*) You're quite sure? (*She listens*) I see. (*She listens*) Very well, send a full written statement immediately, without fail, please. Good night. (*She puts down the receiver and turns to the anxious group*) That was Mrs Newcastle. She's found her fur.

(*The others are so amazed that for a moment they stare in blank astonishment. Then all, except Hattie, speak at once*)

BEE			The wicked old sinner!
LILY			Found it?
ALICE	}	(*together*) {	How dare she!
BRIGADIER			You mean all this is a mistake?

WILSON (*moving to* C) She evidently hid it in a drawer for safety, and forgot.
BEE. I shall sue her for false pretences.
BRIGADIER. Does it mean that this shameless persecution is at an end?
WILSON. It does, sir. (*Moving to Lily*) I'm sorry I doubted you—

it's just one of those things. (*To the others*) And I apologize for so inconveniencing you and your friends, madam.

BEE (*grandly*) You are forgiven. And have our permission to retire.

WILSON. Thank you. (*Going to the doors*) I shouldn't sue Mrs Newcastle if I were you, madam. (*With a smile*) But I'd certainly give her Hell!

(WILSON *exits to the hall.* LILY *darts and opens the front door, and* WILSON *goes out*)

ALICE (*sitting on the stool*) Oh, the relief!

BRIGADIER (*going to the window*) I thought we'd had it.

BEE. Bless the beloved General Post Office telephone.

LILY (*moving to up* L *of the ottoman*) I don't understand, Dame dear. How did you get the fur back?

BEE (*rising*) Don't be silly—it isn't back. (*She takes it from the ottoman*) Talk about sitting on a volcano . . .

LILY. But I thought you said . . .

(NAN *enters hurriedly through the doors to up* C)

NAN. Saw her leave. Does it mean my phone call worked all right?

LILY. That was you ringing up?

NAN. Of course!

BRIGADIER (*moving to* L *of Nan and ringing her hand*) Beautifully done, beautifully done.

LILY (*to* R *of Nan*) Oh, bless you, bless you.

ALICE. Wonderful.

BEE. You saved us in the nick of time.

NAN. I rang old Mother Newcastle, too. Said I was the police; that a fur like hers had just been brought in and would she come down to the police station immediately.

LILY. But they haven't got it—it's here!

NAN. It's not. (*She goes to Bee, takes the fur, moves to* R *of Lily and gives it to her*) It's in a drawer in her bedroom where you're going to put it while she's down at the station!

LILY (*dashing to the doors*) I'll thank you all for the rest of my life.

(LILY *exits*)

BRIGADIER (*moving and sitting on the ottoman,* L *end*) I need a double whisky after this.

BEE. I'll get us all one. (*She starts to go to the sideboard, then stops*) Oh! I hid the bottle in the clock—Lily was taking nips for Ted. (*She starts to go to the grandfather clock, but suddenly notices Hattie still lying in the chair*) Hattie!

ALICE. I'd forgotten all about her—the poor dear.

(*They all go to her, the* BRIGADIER *to down* C, NAN *up* R *of the armchair,* BEE *to* L *of Nan,* ALICE *to* L *of the armchair*)

BEE. It's all right, Hattie dear. She's gone. You can stop pretending.

(*There is no response from Hattie*)

NAN. Christmas! The poor beast really has fainted.
BEE. No!
ALICE. How awful. My smelling salts! (*She gets her smelling salts from her bag on the stool*)

(*They all fuss round Hattie*)

BRIGADIER. Put her head between her knees.
BEE. She's coming round.
HATTIE (*opening her eyes*) Where am I? In prison?
ALICE. No, no, dear—with us, and everything's all right.
HATTIE (*slightly hysterical*) It was terrible, absolutely terrible.
BRIGADIER. It's all over now.
HATTIE. But we were so nearly caught. It was the writing on the wall. We must stop!
NAN (*sadly*) The poor beast's right, you know.
ALICE. Yes, I'm afraid it's got too big for us.
BEE. Furs are so bulky and difficult.
BRIGADIER. We can't possibly stop.
HATTIE (*hysterically*) Yes, yes we must! Promise! Promise, all of you, that we'll never have anything to do with furs of any sort ever again ever.
BRIGADIER. But, Hatfield . . .
HATTIE (*rising and almost screaming*) I shall go to the police myself and confess all if you don't! I shall!
BEE (*sadly shaking her head*) She's hysterical, but she's right. (*She puts Hattie back in the chair*) I promise. (*She sits on the stool below the table*)
NAN (*sadly; going and sitting C on the ottoman*) So do I.
ALICE (*sadly; sitting in the desk chair*) And I.
BRIGADIER. Well, I can't carry on by myself. (*Regretfully shaking his head and sitting on the L end of the ottoman*) But what a terrible decision.

(*They all sit gloomily*)

No more parcels for anyone . . .
ALICE (*sadly shaking her head*) No delighted faces in the Cromwell Road . . .
NAN. It's a damnable shame.
BEE (*sighing*) We'll all have a whisky. (*She goes over to the clock, opens the door and puts her hand down inside. Puzzled*) Hullo! What's this? (*She takes out a large ball of crumpled newspaper*)
NAN. Something hidden in the clock?
BEE. Yes. Very odd. It certainly wasn't there when I hid the whisky.

HATTIE (*rising excitedly*) The man I saw last night! The burglar!
ALICE (*rising*) Quickly—look and see what it is.

(BEE *opens the paper and peers in. Then she looks up at them in amazed
excitement. The* BRIGADIER *and* NAN *rise*)

BRIGADIER (*catching her mood*) What is it, Beatrice, what is it?

(BEE *comes down* C, *to* L *of the Brigadier*)

BEE (*with shining eyes*) Delighted faces in the Cromwell Road!

Smiling happily, BEE *opens the paper and shows the contents; a heap
of shining jewellery, including a flashing tiara which she holds up and
waves. Their faces light up in delighted expectation, as*—

the CURTAIN *falls*

FURNITURE AND PROPERTY LIST

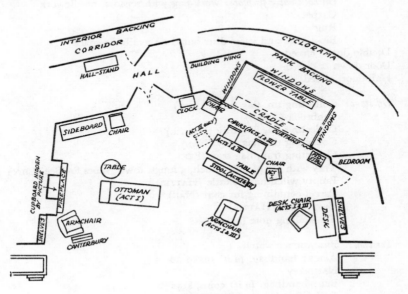

ACT I

On stage : Ottoman. *On it :* 3 cushions

Small armchair (down R) *On it :* 2 cushions, small rug

Tub chair (LC) *On it :* cushion

Dining table. *On it :* map of West End on pile of books, mounted on drawing-board

4 small matching chairs

2 elbow chairs

Sideboard. *On it :* lamp

Grandfather clock

Pedestal with bust and concealed cupboard in plinth

Plant table with various plants

3 hanging plants

Desk. *On it :* blotter, inkstand, penholder, calendar, pencils, telephone, lamp, envelopes, handbell, ashtray

Occasional table (above ottoman) *On it :* cooking ringer, clipboard, pen

Stool. *On it :* collecting tins, flag trays

Canterbury. *In it : The Times*, other newspapers, magazines

Cosy-stove

Hallstand. *On it:* silk coat, hat
Over fireplace: hinged picture concealing cupboard
In bay window: watering-can, binoculars, wooden cradle on
    pulleys concealed by pelmet
On hook above fireplace: work-bag with scissors, needlework
Carpet
Rug
Bic-a-brac and vases distributed on available space
Double doors, closed
Door down L, closed
Hall door, closed

Off stage: Collecting tin, flag tray (ALICE)
Umbrella (ALICE)
Collecting tin, flag tray (HATTIE)
Collecting tin, flag tray (NAN)
Collecting tray, flag tray (BEE)
Tray with jug of rum punch, 5 mugs, towel, shoes for Bee (LILY)
Empty witch-hazel bottle (HATTIE)
Parcel containing fur coat (NAN)
Two letters (HATTIE)
Ten-shilling note (LILY)

Personal: BRIGADIER: watch
ALICE: handbag. *In it:* make-up
NAN: key
BEE: handbag. *In it:* coins, keys
LILY: watch, ten-shilling note
MIKE: handkerchief
        notecase with ten-pound notes

ACT II

Strike: Maps, books, collecting tins, trays
Mugs
Tray and jug
Fur coat
Brown paper and string
Witch-hazel bottle

Check: Doors closed

Set: Ottoman at sharper angle to floats
   Dining table level with floats
Desk chair to L of table
2 small chairs above it
Chair to R of it
Stool below it
Armchair from LC to desk
Chair in window bay
In cushion on armchair down R: 2 bundles of ten-pound notes
In ottoman: 2 Persian lamb coats
On dining table: cloth, 6 coffee-cups and saucers, spoons, croissants,
  butter, marmalade, coffee-pot, milk jug, sugar basin, napkins,
  medicine bottle and spoon, 9 opened letters
Below fire: parsol with key in trick handle
In bookshelves: book with list inside
On desk: pencil. *In drawer:* notebook with pencil, monocle, lace scarf
On ottoman table: clipboard and pen
On hook: work-bag

In cupboard over fireplace : duster, polish, false number card, false name card

In pedestal : bank statement

Off stage : Stole (HATTIE)
Hoover box (CHRIS)
Screwdriver, hammer (TED)
Apron, maid's cap, steel glasses (BEE)
Dark glasses, scarves, gloves (HATTIE)

Personal : BRIGADIER: whistle on lanyard, watch
CHRIS: ten-pound notes
TED: penknife, matches
NAN: handkerchief
MADAME CHAMBERT: handbag. *In it :* cheque-book, pen, order to view

ACT III

Strike : Everything off table except cloth
Binoculars
Duster and polish
Stole

Set : Table LC to original position
2 chairs above table
Chair to R of table
Stool below table
Desk chair and armchair LC to original positions
On table LC: piles of pound notes, sealed envelopes, clean envelopes, pen, exercise book
On desk : vase of flowers
In grandfather clock : jewellery, including tiara, in old newspaper
On table above ottoman : cigarettes, lighter, ashtray
In ottoman : white ermine cape
On stool : Alice's handbag with make-up and smelling-salts
In bookshelves : book containing 2 snapshots

Check : Window curtains drawn
Doors closed

Off stage : 2 violin cases containing 1 fur each (NAN)
French horn case containing 1 fur (NAN)
French horn case containing 2 furs (NAN)
Tuba case containing fur (MIKE)

Personal : BRIGADIER: medals, watch, concert tickets, coin
HATTIE: key (supposedly taken from Mike)

LIGHTING PLOT

Property fittings required: fire brackets, 2 table lamps, hall pendant
  Interior. A sitting-room. The same scene throughout
  THE APPARENT SOURCE OF LIGHT, in daytime, is a bay window up R;
    at night, lamps and brackets
  THE MAIN ACTING AREAS are down R, RC, C and LC

ACT I. Afternoon

To open: Effect of rainy afternoon
        Lamps and brackets off
        Hall pendant on

No cues

ACT II. Morning

To open: Effect of morning sunlight
        Lamps and brackets off
        Hall pendant on

Cue 1   BEE switches off hall pendant   (Page 45)
        Take out hall pendant

ACT III. Evening

To open: Blue in floods outside window
        Lamps brackets and pendant on

Cue 2   HATTIE switches off lights   (Page 57)
        Snap out all interior lighting

Cue 3   HATTIE switches on lights   (Page 57)
        Snap on all interior lighting

EFFECTS PLOT

ACT I

ACT III

Any character costumes or wigs needed in the performance of this play
can be hired from Charles H. Fox Ltd, 184 High Holborn, London W.C.1

MADE AND PRINTED IN GREAT BRITAIN BY
LATIMER TREND AND CO. LTD, WHITSTABLE
MADE IN ENGLAND